MAINE MAN
The Tony Book Story

Tony Book is now honorary president at Manchester City Football Club and still lives in Manchester.

David Clayton is the editor of the Manchester City Magazine, the club's official publication, writes for the *Manchester Evening News* and has contributed to *The Guardian*. He is also the author of *Everything Under the Blue Moon*, *The Little Book of Man City* and *Blue Blood*.

MAINSTREAM / SPORT

MAINE MAN

THE TONY BOOK STORY

TONY BOOK AND DAVID CLAYTON

MAINSTREAM
PUBLISHING
EDINBURGH AND LONDON

This edition, 2005

First published in Great Britain in 2004 by
MAINSTREAM PUBLISHING COMPANY (EDINBURGH) LTD
7 Albany Street
Edinburgh EH1 3UG

ISBN 1 84596 039 4

A catalogue record for this book is available from the British Library

Typeset in Baskerville Book and Century Gothic
Printed and bound in Great Britain by
Cox & Wyman Ltd

For Sylvia, Tracey, Anthony and all the family
Tony Book

For you, Mum
David Clayton

Contents

Acknowledgements

I would like to thank the following people: my wife Sylvia, daughter Tracey and son Anthony Book for their unwavering support for me over the years. I was 30 years old when Tracey was born, and Anthony followed not too long after. Their childhood directly coincided with my professional football career – first as a player, and then as a manager – and Sylvia brought them up while I took on the role of the breadwinner. This meant that I wasn't there for them all the time, and there isn't a day that goes by that I wish I had been.

I am also deeply indebted to my mother, father and my six brothers, who have supported me throughout my life. I recall how proud they all were when Manchester City got to the FA Cup final in 1969, and all of them (except my brother, Rodney, who was serving in the Army) travelled from Bath to Wembley to see me play. With backing like that, you just can't fail, can you?

Thanks, too, to all my mates in Bath – especially John Swift and Brian Barnes – who have always stuck by me and followed my career so enthusiastically.

I'm forever indebted to Malcolm Allison, who was the one who gave me a chance and then fought to get me to Maine Road. He has provided one of the forewords for this book, despite not being in the best of health, and I am extremely grateful to him for that. I am equally indebted to Joe Mercer, who was a father figure when I first joined the club. Thanks to Ian McFarlane, for helping me get off to such a good start as a manager, and to the late Bill Taylor, for helping me to carry on where Ian had left off.

A big thanks, too, to the City fans for their constant support down the years. So many expressed their sorrow when I was sacked and I thank each and every one of them for their letters and kind words.

My special thanks to David Clayton, co-writer of this tome, for his expertise, patience, understanding and constant support in the production of this book. Sincere thanks, also, to his wife Sarah and his young family for allowing him the time to do it.

Finally, I'd like to express my gratitude to Colin Bell for writing the first of this book's two forewords. What more could you ask of a friend? We are both quiet types, and perhaps this is why we'd always got on so well together at City. He's one of the club's greatest players and I'm grateful to have his words opening my story.

Tony Book

I would like to thank Tony Book for the opportunity of helping him to bring his life story to print. This is the second autobiography I've assisted on, and both have been a privilege. Tony's is a fascinating tale that reminded me of the *Roy of the Rovers* stories I occasionally read as a kid. It was Boys' Own stuff and is perhaps unique in the history of British football. I feel sure his path to greatness will never be repeated, and to have the chance to get to know one of the club's greatest players and managers is ample reward for all the late nights that go into compiling a book. I would also like to thank his wife, Sylvia, for all her hospitality over the past 18 months. Tony and Sylvia are a lovely couple, and it's not hard to see why they've been married for more than 45 years. They might speak in that gentle West Country accent but they are as Mancunian as anyone I know.

I am also indebted to Bill Campbell, Graeme Blaikie and Lizzie Cameron at Mainstream Publishing, Edinburgh. Thanks for the continuing support and belief, Bill, and congratulations to you and Sharon on the recent birth of your daughter. Thanks to Graeme for the flexible deadline and for being as laid-back as ever – it helps a lot! Great cover design by Lizzie, and thanks, too, to the *Manchester Evening News* for the use of the stunning image of Tony lighting up a cigarette shortly before being relieved of the manager's job at Maine Road.

Thanks to Brian Barnes and Rheece Book, for their early memories of Tony. It was a pleasure to finally meet Malcolm Allison, though his surroundings left me saddened. He is the greatest coach Manchester City have ever had, and he deserves better. Maybe we can all rally together to show our appreciation of his past achievements.

Finally, a big hug and kisses to my wife Sarah, and my two beautiful children, Harry and Jaimé – a right pair of rascals – for putting up with all those late nights and lost weekends.

David Clayton

FOREWORD

by Colin Bell

I've been friends with Tony Book for more than 38 years, from our time together at Maine Road up to the present day. I remember when he first arrived at City from Plymouth Argyle and, in all honesty, I wondered why they had bought a player of his age. But Malcolm Allison knew him well and had been with him at Bath City and Plymouth Argyle, so he obviously knew what he was doing. When I first saw him, I thought, 'Just how old is he?' I'd just signed from Bury as a fresh-faced 19 year old and I knew the club were trying to build for the future, but I couldn't work out why they'd brought someone in who was surely nearing the end of his career.

Tony, however, turned out to be probably the best pound-for-pound signing City ever made. I think he cost around £17,000 and, for the service and years we got out of him, he was great value for money. It wasn't too long before Malcolm made Tony captain, a job I believe he'd had at his last two clubs, and to all the lads it made perfect sense because he had the total respect of all his teammates and always set the standard for others to match in training.

He was 32 when he first arrived, and he knew he had to stay at the peak of fitness to extend his career as long as possible. He looked after himself well and was totally dedicated – and still is – to Manchester City. He would return to pre-season training three weeks before the rest of the squad and train on his own until we all came back from our break, and then he'd join in with the rest of us. Then, when we'd finished the session, he'd carry on with a bit of gym work or weights for a couple of hours.

His level of dedication undoubtedly rubbed off on the rest of the squad because, on top of the respect we all had for him, here was a man who, despite being older than all the other players, looked after himself and was prepared to work harder than anyone else. In addition to all of this, of course, Tony Book was a born winner.

Sometimes I used to wonder how we turned out a full eleven players each Saturday, because every Friday we had a match – defence versus forwards – and Skip, as we all called him, was one of the men who used to kick lumps out of you! In the defenders' side there were Tony, Mike Doyle, Glyn Pardoe and Alan Oakes, and none of them would pull out of anything with the tackles flying in. Tony didn't know how to give less than 100 per cent. Whether it was in a practice match or a League game, he just didn't know any different. He was completely dedicated to winning, and Manchester City Football Club was his life.

Another side to his personality was that he was a bad loser, and I love to have people like that playing around me. When I look back at the team we had, they were all bad losers, but that was perhaps something none of us appreciated until much later on. Tony didn't just want to win every game he played in but also to win every tackle he made, and every other challenge he was involved in, during a game and it definitely rubbed off on us all. He was the perfect man to lead the team – his attitude was spot on and he expected everyone else to give the same as he did.

I didn't see too much of him when he became manager because I was injured for much of the time and off training on my own or on the treatment table. All the lads who played regularly under him said he was a very good manager and no doubt he'd picked up a lot from Malcolm and Joe along the way. It was Tony, however, who picked me as substitute on Boxing Day 1977 and then asked me to go out for the second half after I'd been out almost two years with injury. It was great management, because the fantastic reception I was given seemed to lift the supporters up and the rest of the team, too. It might have been a bad move in that they were carrying me somewhat with my injured leg, but we went on to win 4–0 after being held 0–0 at the break. That was the first of seven successive wins and it kick-started the season, which was all credit to Tony's skills as a manager.

We've always been close friends and, from the moment he stepped through the main entrance at Maine Road to the present day, Tony Book's life has been dedicated to Manchester City. He absolutely adores the club and, like me, he's got Blue blood. We may not have been born in Manchester, but neither of us could ever imagine living anywhere else, and I can't think of a better ambassador for the club than Tony.

Colin Bell,
Hale Barns, March 2004

FOREWORD

by Malcolm Allison

The first time I saw Tony Book was shortly after I'd been given the job as manager of Bath City. I had to climb scaffolding to meet him, so he began life in an elevated position with me and ended even higher. The first time I saw him play I thought he was rubbish . . . of course, I'm only joking. Out of all the players I coached in my career, Tony was my favourite – and I mean favourite. He had everything a good footballer needs. Many players have a lot of great attributes but Tony had the lot. He was with me at Bath, and when I invited him over to play in Canada for the summer he played exceptionally well – but then, he never let me down. He was a wonderful athlete and the consummate professional.

Football managers go through their lives seeking the perfect professional, a man they can trust, whose example and attitude sets exactly the right tone in a dressing room. I found that man at Bath City, and the first decision I made when I left for Plymouth Argyle was to go back to Bath for Tony. I recall a director laughing when I gave him a cheque for £1,500. He thought I was mad, paying that money for someone who was past his 30th birthday, but I knew the value of Tony Book, and when I moved to Manchester City I instinctively signed him again.

He should have played for England. Even in his mid-30s he was as quick and as sharp as any player in the country, and his reading of defensive situations was simply brilliant. It's impossible to calculate precisely his contribution to the Blues as the team powered through the trophy-winning years but, believe me, it was very high.

Off the pitch, we did our own thing but I reckon he didn't live the same life as me because he couldn't afford to keep up with me! He was a tremendous captain and I think he got better each week. People used to say to me, 'You know how old he is, don't you?' That was the first thing anybody said about him and I used to say, 'I know exactly how old he is – always have done – and you don't change in age much from week to week, do you?' He had the pace of a teenager and his age was never a problem to me. It didn't matter to me one jot and I had a few arguments about it with various people down the years, too. I made him captain at all the clubs I was at and, of course, gave him a few quid extra in the process.

He went on to become a good manager, and when people ask me if I thought he had taken anything from the way I used to coach the team, I'd tell them, 'No, but I took a few pointers off Tony!' The best thing about Tony is that he is the same bloke today as he was when I first met him at Bath – he's never changed from that day to this. That I brought Tony into League football is one of the great satisfactions of my career, but I take no credit for it. It took no great insight, no wild hunches to see that he had a lot to offer at the very top of the game. He has never been in my debt. Whatever faith I showed in him he has repaid many times over.

I was born to coach and Tony was born to play. That's the way it was.

Malcolm Allison,
Sale, March 2004

Introduction

I wanted to write this book and tell my story because of the uniqueness of my path into top-flight football. The way things are today, it's hard to see it ever happening again. Can you really see a Premiership club taking on a 32 year old who played most of his career in non-League football?

Lifting the Division One championship trophy and winning a major European cup were a million miles away from my humble beginnings a stone's throw from Bath City's ground. In fact, for the first 30 years of my life, there was not so much as the merest hint that my football career would include anything other than Southern League football for my home-town club and working for Mortimers, a building firm that took on most of the council work in and around the Bath area. I had all but accepted that my opportunities had dried up and the fact that I was approaching the age when most players begin to consider a future away from football lengthened my odds of success considerably. I was facing years of dark mornings on building sites, often in cold, miserable conditions, working in trenches and building the foundations for flats and houses and, when the football ended, I would be left with a job I didn't particularly enjoy as my sole source of income. The thought sends a shiver down my spine even now. The amount of times I had to go out at the crack of dawn to shovel snow for the council in mid-winter with my bones aching and hands and feet frozen doesn't bear thinking about, and this was at a time when I was at my physical peak, too. As I advanced in years, it would have got much harder and who knows what might have happened? Maybe I would have become a foreman, and maybe not. I worked hard in the building game throughout my time at Bath City and this, more than anything else, highlights the difference between making it in football and nearly making it. At this stage, I was squarely in the latter category.

Sometimes, however, strange things happen and if any phrase fitted my life perfectly, it would have to be 'Good things come to those who wait'. I waited and the good things came, thick and fast. Perhaps, in a parallel universe, there is another Tony Book, still shovelling snow and dreaming of retirement and wondering what might have been had he been given the chance to show what he could do whilst he was playing. If you ever come across him, tell him not to get too downhearted because it doesn't matter what age you are, it really is never too late to realise your dreams. I should know . . .

ONE

Indian Signs

I was born on 4 September 1934 in the Somerset spa town of Bath and was one of what would eventually be a total of seven boys. My dad was an Army man for most of his adult life, joining as a boy entrant to the Somerset Light Infantry, and would stay in the military for 34 years, all told. Of course, that wasn't destined to be the life for me but in later years I too would serve my time for Queen and country.

Charlie Book, my father, was posted to India, which meant our family uprooting to Asia to live for what would be a total of seven years. At the time, I was only four and the youngest child in the family. Along with my two older brothers, I took the move to foreign lands in my stride. The cold English winters under leaden grey skies were about to be replaced by heat, humidity and endless sunshine as we set sail from Southampton in December 1938 for a new life. I can recall feeling like Phileas Fogg setting out on a wonderful adventure as the boat left the dock and I stood holding my mum's hand, watching the land shrink further away until we were surrounded only by ocean. The ship that would be our home for a while was a troop ship, and that meant my father wasn't allowed to sleep with us because of the segregation the Army demanded. We spent Christmas at sea and our voyage lasted for around six weeks, which is an age for any young kid, but I entertained myself as best I could, playing games with my brothers and reading comics. The biggest concern for my mother were the low rails around the ship and the thought of me toppling over into the icy waters below, but I never strayed too far away.

We finally arrived and started our new life in India. Over the course of the next seven years, it was England and its people that would become foreign to me as I effectively grew up an Indian boy. Yet British people surrounded me throughout our stay and, I hasten to add, we were treated like royalty for most of our time there, thanks to Dad's status in the military. Because we were white skinned and British, we could wander around without anyone bothering us. In fact, the local people couldn't do enough for us. After arriving at Bombay, we moved to Phuna, some 3,000 feet above sea level, high up in the mountains and close to the city of Davangere.

We had not been in India long before Dad was posted to Burma to fight for the British Army and, together with my mother and two brothers, Rheece and Mervyn, we were left with other officers' families to settle and acclimatise to our new way of life. While the war raged on, we were treated extremely well and even had servants in our home – which could be a house, apartment or tent, depending on where we were based. As a youngster, I began mixing with local children, often the youngsters of the servants and it was around this time that I started to play football – of sorts!

The 'ball' in question was a rolled-up collection of rags, bonded together with God-knows-what but it did the trick. After all, it wasn't as if my mum could nip down to J.D. Sports to get me a new Mitre football, so we improvised as best we could, though in some of the camps we lived in there was the odd 'real' ball here and there. My brothers and I played barefoot on any flat expanse of dirt we could find and had knockabouts with the local kids. The soles of our feet were soon as hard as nails but, as skin was the chosen 'footwear', it was the done thing. It wasn't only football that we played on those long, hot Indian summer days – there was hockey and cricket, too. I can't ever remember feeling bored in all the time I was there. There was also a racetrack nearby and we occasionally wandered up to watch the horses or take in a game of football in the local stadium, which was a fair size. There was always a match of some kind going on in there.

Some of the children from the local villages would take me out with a catapult to shoot pellets at lizards and snakes – just teasing the unfortunate beasts, you understand, and no animal was ever killed or wounded on the rare occasions when we actually hit the poor devils. The Indian kids could speak a little English and we learned a little Hindustani, too. When you're that age, of course, you have your own language that you seem to get by just fine with. Most of the local community were extremely poor and lived in appalling conditions. Sanitation in the villages was virtually non-existent, with open sewers alongside the dirt roads. For health reasons alone we weren't allowed to go too far into the local populace and were told to stay fairly close to the Army camps.

I soon learned of the local wildlife and the species I had to keep well away from. There was a plethora of poisonous serpents, spiders, scorpions and various other creepy-crawlies that could have been potentially fatal, in India. Fortunately, the only snakes that we came into close contact with were the harmless grass snakes that hid near the concrete base of the huge tents that we sometimes lived in. Bigger animals such as elephants were around but they were under their handlers' control. Sadly, I can't recall ever taking the opportunity to take a ride on one – I wasn't too comfortable with heights at that time! Hyenas and tigers were close by in the mountains but we didn't go looking for them and, thankfully, they never came looking for us. We knew they were out there and that was enough to keep us on our toes.

In fact, the wildest beasts on four legs to venture near our camp were the nanny goats that the locals allowed to graze on the green lawns around the base. We'd try to catch them to get some milk but they usually shook us off with ease. The food we ate wasn't exactly the roast beef and Yorkshire pudding of home – not that I noticed that much, being so young – but my family soon learned to love the curries the cook prepared and the endless varieties of exotic fruits and vegetables that were served up. We'd eat with our hands like the locals did and it was all very enjoyable and exactly what most kids do, given the chance, anyway. When in India . . . as the saying goes.

The hired-help around the house certainly made things easier for my mother. The servants would do pretty much everything and, in truth, it wasn't a bad life for a British woman in India, especially the wife of a captain quartermaster. In fact, we had the best of everything. During our stay, there were two more additions to the Book family – two more babies were born on Indian soil, making my mum and dad the proud parents of five boys. Not only did we now officially have enough players for our own five-a-side team, this also proved that my mum and dad did occasionally see each other during the war!

The endless heat, humidity and sunshine, however – interrupted only now and then by the occasional monsoon – was beginning to have a detrimental effect on my health, though it took a while to work out exactly what it was. We moved around India a lot during our stay, starting off in Phuna, Multaan, then Bombay; from there up to Harihar and then on to Karachi, travelling on packed trains from place to place. It was in Bombay that my health problems really began to affect my everyday activities. Having moved into an apartment, we were now living on the fourth floor and that meant climbing a number of stairs, as there were no lifts to use. I found myself going up the first flight of stairs and having to sit down and get my breath back. For a supposedly fit young boy to have difficulty breathing after the briefest exertion, it could only mean one thing – asthma – though the Army doctor failed to diagnose the condition. It was only my mum's persistence that resulted in me seeing an Indian doctor who prescribed some medication that eased the problem. I would get home and need to lie down, which was not something a young kid should have to do, but I had no other choice, having no inhaler to open my airways up. Despite all the ills and ailments associated with living in Britain's damp climate, it was a problem that would leave me for good the moment we returned to England, and it has never troubled me since.

We moved around a lot but always seemed to return to Phuna. It was while we were on one of our several stays there that my brother, Rheece, believes I finally began to take more than just a passing interest in football. The military barracks we'd lived in previously had been turned into an Army hospital. A number of Italian prisoners of war worked there as orderlies, and many of them would have a knock-around near their barracks. After a while, I joined in. I was aged about seven at the time and maybe the Italians' natural defensive instincts began to rub off on me and have more effect than I've ever given them credit for.

Bolton Wanderers star Bobby Langton was also stationed where we were staying for a while and, naturally, I was delighted. I wanted to be around someone who'd played the game at that level and who might even be called up for England (although this did not end up happening). I used to go and have a kick-about with him and my brothers and he would help me with all the basics. He'd tell me to kick the ball against a wall and learn how to trap it and control it. These are two very basic, but fundamental, skills that you need in football, and the earlier you can do them, the better. People say practice makes perfect but I believed practice makes permanent – the more practice you put in, the better, and those skills don't go away once you've acquired them.

The worst thing about our stay in India was my father's active military service in Burma. There was a bloody war raging with the Burmese and you could never be sure if Father would ever return safely from battle. He was away for eighteen months at one point and I witnessed families being informed that their father would never be coming back. I dreaded a telegram bearing terrible news being delivered to my mother but you had to learn to live with it. This was the British Empire and it was expected. It was the days of the stiff upper lip and life had to go on. Thank God my dad made it out safely, having said all that.

We stayed in India for two more years after Dad had served his time attached to the Indian Army in the Royal Army Medical Corps. I was 11 years old by the time we set sail for Southampton in September 1945 for our return journey, passing through the magnificent Suez Canal along the way. Being away from Britain for so long meant that we had missed World War Two entirely. The atom bomb had been dropped on Hiroshima and Asia was finished as far as the military were concerned. My mother was pregnant again and was advised not to travel but my father, who had been out in India for so long, was one of the first to be allowed to return home. He must have used his rank in the military to ensure we were on the next available ship back to Southampton. We sailed back to England first class on a Dutch cruise ship. There were British prisoners of war that had been held captive in Japan on board, too, but we didn't see them very often. My childhood had been spent a world away from kids of my own age back home and, when we finally set sail for the lengthy trip back, I began to wonder what state my birth country would be in. I knew from relatives that Bath had come through the war relatively unscathed in comparison with most of the major cities up and down England, and we had been lucky that we hadn't lost any family members during our time away. I knew of Hitler and the Nazis but didn't experience the togetherness and spirit of defeating the Germans that the rest of the country had.

We finally arrived back home in the winter of 1945 and moved into 22 Innox Road, Twerton, Bath – home of my mum's sister, Aunt Maud – just a stone's throw from Bath City's Twerton Park home ground, which would become a big part of my life in future years. Maud and her husband, Ted, had three kids of their own and there were seven in our party so, as you can imagine, it was pretty cramped! We stayed for around two months until things got unbearably cluttered and Mum and Dad knew we couldn't function as a family any more, living the way we were – we just had to find our own place. The first school I went to was a local secondary modern called West Twerton. I was at an age where I was between schools, and I could have gone to a primary school for a year but it made more sense that I started at a level which I wouldn't have to leave within a year. I began to play football again, but this time with real leather footballs and the appropriate and approved footwear. It felt a little strange at first but I soon got used to it, as I began to settle down in what still seemed like a foreign place to me. Having said that, I still used to play barefoot in the parks shortly after our return and did as well as anyone playing in boots or trainers. I didn't keep this up for long, however, and only did it on the warmer days.

I was only a short, lightly built lad but I did OK in the school matches where I played as inside-forward. The bigger lads were invariably picked ahead of me but my father wasn't having any of it. He was, if anything, over-keen to see me progress and play in the team. If I was left on the sidelines, he'd talk with the teachers to try to influence their selection and it came to a point where I had to tell him not to, because without him realising, it was hindering me and also a little embarrassing.

'If I'm going to make my way in this game, Dad, you've got to leave it to me,' I told him. He understood and, though his support never wavered, he did as I asked and took a step back. West Twerton had a very good sports master called Fred Lease, who wasn't overly concerned about my size and gave me the opportunity to show what I was capable of. He took us for many sports, including basketball, and also held some enjoyable three-a-side sessions for the football team in the gymnasium on Saturday nights, with benches for the goals. It was a wonderful time.

With my Indian background, I seemed to be of great interest to the other kids at West Twerton. They looked at me a little oddly in the early days, when I still had dark skin. It was a council house area and a tight-knit community, so when word got around that we'd moved to Bath from India, I think they probably expected a genuine Indian family. It was just curiosity and a bit of a novelty for them at the time but I was treated the same as everybody else and there were no problems. I soon made plenty of friends, many of whom wanted to hear about my adventures in India. I think my father's status in the Army helped, as a certain amount of respect seemed to be given to the whole family.

I did progress well at schoolboy level and soon made the Bath boys' side and then the Somerset representative team, too. I knew I had a little bit of ability but, because of my size, I honestly never thought I'd get on in the game. As I was keen to play as much football as I could, I joined an additional team, Peasedown Miners Youth, which was based in a nearby village. Peasedown Miners were a Western League side and it would be the beginning of a long association with the club that would also eventually lead me to meet my future wife – but more of that later on. Dad remained a regular soldier for the first two years of our return as we acclimatised back to English life. My mum, meanwhile, was finding life tough after eight years of being waited upon hand and foot. There were also another two additions to our family unit, with the arrival of two more brothers. Imagine my poor mum running around after seven boys! Needless to say, our aunt's house had finally been vacated. We'd found our own home at Oldfield Park with much-needed space. It was still a little cramped, being only a three-bedroomed terrace, but it felt a lot roomier than the slightly overcrowded dwelling we'd been in since our return.

It was now 1951. I was 16 years old and I'd left West Twerton School. I can't say I was a fantastic scholar but I did excel in sports, enjoying gymnastics as well as football and cricket. I suppose I was as mischievous as any lad my age was and would often play 'knock-up ginger' with my best school pal and someone I still speak with every week to the present day, Brian Barnes. We'd tie a string to a doorknocker and hide behind a hedge, then pull the string to knock on the door. When the people used to answer the door we'd let the string drop to the ground so they couldn't see it and then knock again when they closed the door. The person we'd been tormenting would occasionally chase us and every now and then the local policeman, a big bloke called Sergeant Ledger, would catch us on his bike and give us a stinging clip around the ear and tell us not to do it again, but, of course, we would.

When we weren't annoying the local residents, it would be football in the park with a group of mates. Sundays were the best because the older lads who were working the rest of the week would join in for a game. There'd be 15- or 16-a-side, and with so many other lads involved you wouldn't see the ball too often so when you did, you had to make the most of it. I had a strong will to win – even back then – and it would occasionally end in scraps with other lads and even my best mate Brian on one or two of our less agreeable days. I enjoyed getting stuck in against the bigger lads and I certainly didn't mind the physical side of the game. Maybe it was my size that added the extra fire to my belly but, whatever it was, I was determined to show I could mix it with the best of them. I must admit, determination is something of a family trait.

I'd saunter down to watch Bath City every now and then, and sometimes I'd go to watch Bristol City or Bristol Rovers as well. The Somerset area was hardly a soccer hotbed in terms of football talent and successful League teams but the interest was there all the same. I began working in a local Co-op shop with my mate Brian and it was around this time that I discovered the dubious delights of the cigarette. I'd sweep up the sawdust from the floor every now and then and either Brian or myself would 'accidentally' knock a few of the cigarettes, which were stacked loosely, onto the floor and sweep them away with the sawdust. We'd end up with a dozen or so fags and inevitably I was hooked from an early age. With a limitless, free supply, was it any wonder?

I continued to play for Peasedown Miners and played in numerous local derbies against the likes of Clandown, Radstock and Paulton as an inside-forward. Amongst the sparse crowds that came to watch us play was a crowd of girls who used to come from the local village of Peasedown St John. There was one occasion when I took over in goal after our goalkeeper was injured. I certainly wasn't built like a goalkeeper, and with my oversize green jersey on and legs like pipe cleaners I suppose I was asking for trouble! The girls were behind my goal and they were teasing me about my legs. I caught the attention of one of the girls – Sylvia, as I later found out – and kept shaking my head at her every time the goals flew past me into the net. I couldn't concentrate properly but it was all in good fun.

I began to date Sylvia after this, though I doubt either of us imagined we would spend the rest of our lives together, especially after the ribbing I'd taken for my legs!

TWO

Pensioned Off by Chelsea

'You'll make the grade, Tony. I'll write to my boss and tell him about you. I'm convinced you've got the ability to be a First Division player.'

Ex-Chelsea winger Frank Blunstone

The 1950s may have been an exciting time in America and Britain but I was concentrating on one thing – football. I now knew I had enough ability to make a living of sorts in the game but I wasn't sure where exactly my future lay. There was also the prospect of national service looming on the horizon. It was an accepted part of life back then and, coming from a family with a strong military background, it held few fears for me, although I admit it was never going to be the path I would follow. I was still working with Brian Barnes and Gordon Maggs at the Co-op but it was beginning to interfere with my football because I was working Saturdays until one o'clock in the afternoon. There were many times on a Saturday I'd offer to do the deliveries on my bike. I'd drop off the orders and head off to play at Peasedown, hiding my bike under a hedge along the way until the Monday morning. I was about 17 years old and doing well for the youth team, and I didn't want my Co-op job to hinder my progress. I wanted to be free and available to play every Saturday, without fail. Something had to give, and if it was a choice between serving cooked meat to old ladies or running around a football pitch for ninety minutes giving my all, there was only going to be one winner. At least the cigarette stocks at the Co-op returned to normal levels again when I left and, so far as I am aware, the sales of half-pound portions of roast ham and pork never suffered in my absence.

I still had to earn a real living, so I began an apprenticeship with a building firm in Bath called Mortimers. They did a lot of work for the council and had a good reputation in the town, so I was pleased that they took me on as a bricklayer, especially as my Saturdays were now free again. I'd broken into Peasedown Miners' first team by then and they weren't a bad side to learn my trade with, at least at amateur level. I looked on my time there as another type of apprenticeship. There were always scouts from Bristol Rovers and Bristol City knocking around but nothing positive happened on that front – at least not to me, anyway. Saying that, though, Bristol Rovers did offer me the opportunity of joining them on a training camp in pre-season. They used to stay under canvas on the beaches of Weston-super-Mare and Clevedon but I didn't fancy it at the time. I was hoping something better would come along and was happy to continue my grounding in the lower leagues for a while.

At Mortimers, I began to learn the art of laying bricks under the expert guidance of my mentor Ken Nippard. I wasn't the quickest brickie around, but Ken – who'd been in the game for donkey's years – wasn't too fussed as long as I did a good job. 'Whatever you do, my son,' he'd say in a thick West Country accent, 'keep them upright.' He was a good bloke and I enjoyed being around him and learning from him, as well as listening to his wise old tales. We'd work all over the place – Bath, Bristol, Frome, wherever – building houses, shops and garages, and I soon discovered that I had got over my childhood fear of heights. My driving skills were, on the other hand, an entirely different matter and I had a lot of explaining to do after I drove a wagon into a ditch on a site in Bristol after telling the gaffer I'd passed my driving test a few months earlier. It took a tractor to pull the wagon out and save my bacon, and Ken had a few stern words for me when he found out what I'd been up to. This was an enjoyable time for me, and I felt completely at home. I thought that if my football career didn't take off, there were far worse trades I could have chosen. The winter mornings were tough, but at that age you don't really feel the cold, do you?

My family and I had now moved into a big old house made from the finest Bath stone, on Upper Bristol Road. My eldest brother, Rheece, was always away, having followed in Dad's footsteps in joining the Army, so the house was hardly ever full to capacity. Somebody else was soon to leave the Book household, too – me. My national service papers had arrived, and I was due to start on 21 October 1952. I wondered what effect it would have on my life and future, and how I'd take to the disciplined lifestyle, but I knew what it was all about because of my background, which was more than some of the lads who were drafted at the same time. Like my father had done before me, I applied for the Royal Army Medical Corps and before I knew it I was having my medical and my injections, and getting measured up for my service uniform. My careers at Mortimers and Peasedown Miners would have to be put on hold, though I wasn't sure how much either would miss me.

I was based for my first six weeks of Army life at Fleet in Hampshire, and I was soon mucking in: scrubbing floors and whatever else we were asked to do. After a month of basic training, I took weekend leave and travelled back home to see Sylvia and my family. I was in my full uniform, complete with beret and trench coat, but in truth I felt too ill to leave the barracks and should have stayed in bed for a few days. The problem was I'd been scrubbing floors with dry Vim and it had gone into my throat and chest and I felt awful. My throat was dry and on fire but I was determined to make the journey home. As I walked through the door at home my mother took one look at my ashen face and knew in an instant that I was sick. I spent most of the weekend in bed being looked after – so much for my weekend pass.

Fortunately, that was one of the few low points I can recall and my football connections soon began to make life easier. When I'd completed my training I was moved to a base at Crookham, near Aldershot. With many footballers being drafted to do their service at that time, there was a forces ruling that representative teams should have no more than five professionals and at least six amateurs. It didn't do to have too many good players in a single team, so they were spread amongst the different teams. Because I wasn't a professional, it meant that I had a slightly better chance of making the team for the Royal Army Medical Corps (RAMC), and receiving the few benefits that went along with it. I was selected by Regimental Sergeant-Major (RSM) Tanussi, but not in my preferred position as inside-forward. You didn't get to choose positions, and he just said in the dressing room prior to my first game: 'Book, full-back' and that was that. I'd never even considered playing in defence before but you couldn't argue and just had to get on with it. I'd love to say I became a full-back because it had always been my ambition, but the truth is I was told to play there and couldn't say no!

Ironically, my first-ever game as full-back ended with a red card after I kicked the opposing winger, though it was nothing malicious, just more of a forward's tackle. I took the early bath and didn't think any more about it until I saw my name on the noticeboard the next morning, where a note proclaimed I was to see the commanding officer straight away. I arrived at the designated area and was then frogmarched by the military police to see the CO, but not before they had removed my belt and took my beret off. I felt like I was heading for death row! The CO, a typically brash, imposing figure behind his large desk, was short and sharp with me: 'Book – sent off. Confined to barracks for 14 days. Off you go!' And that was the end of that! I'd had a crash course in Army discipline and I must admit it was a shock to the system. It taught me what was acceptable and what wasn't and, in truth, it probably taught me a lesson that I would never forget. It wouldn't be the last time I was sent off, however, but it brought home the importance of timing the tackles as best you possibly could.

The only time I saw the inside of a hospital during my service in the RAMC was, ironically, when I was the patient! I'd gashed my leg playing football and it'd turned septic, so I'd had to spend a few days in a hospital bed recovering. I had called home to tell them where I was and my mother, who was always slightly over-protective of us all, probably panicked and called my brother up to come and check on how I was. Rheece, who was now a sergeant at Aldershot, rushed across to see me, probably thinking I was at death's door, only to find me sitting up reading a book with a plaster on my knee. It is safe to assume that he wasn't exactly overcome with sympathy for me, as he'd brought not so much as a bunch of grapes to help me to recover.

I continued my service and soon settled into playing at full-back, actually beginning to enjoy my new role. RSM Tanussi had made many contacts throughout football, having dealt with so many drafted players over the past few years, and he seemed to take an interest in my abilities. Chelsea's Frank Blunstone and Trevor Chamberlain of Fulham were in the RAMC at the same time as me and they were allowed to travel back at weekends to play for their clubs. Tanussi arranged for me to have a trial with Chelsea, no less. I travelled to London with Frank on several Wednesday afternoons and had a few games with Chelsea's A-team. I did OK and they seemed quite pleased with me. After a short time, because of Tanussi's connections, I started travelling to Basingstoke on the odd weekend to play for Thorneycroft in the Hampshire League.

I wasn't getting home as much as I would have liked, and poor Sylvia even paid my train fare back to Bath when I wasn't playing football to ensure I made the trip! Even then, I'd turn out for Peasedown Miners when I could. Sylvia knew I was trying to make my way in the game and was always supportive. Perhaps this was partly because it had been football that had brought us together. I was improving all the time because I was playing with experienced professionals in the Army team and I was still on trial with Chelsea. My national service was finally coming to an end, and RSM Tanussi asked Chelsea to make a decision about whether or not they wanted to sign me. I felt I'd done fairly well in the games I had played in and was hopeful that this might be the break I'd been waiting for, but when a letter from the club's manager, Ted Drake, arrived at my home, I sensed the worst and was right. Chelsea had decided they wouldn't stand in my way if I wanted to play football elsewhere and wished me the best of luck in the future. There was to be no contract at Stamford Bridge and no break into League football. I was 20 years old and was heading out of the Army and back to bricklaying and Peasedown Miners. A little downcast, I reckoned this might be my lot in life.

THREE

From Stamford Bridge to Badger's Hill

Back home and free of national service, I began working for Mortimers again. My time at Peasedown Miners, however, was coming to an end. I was offered the chance of moving up a division with Frome Town and, with the added carrot of becoming semi-professional, I took it, of course. It meant more travelling, but my dad used to take me to Badger's Hill – Frome Town's home ground – with Sylvia every week and life was just fine as far as I was concerned. It wasn't Chelsea, but then again I was happy to make any kind of progress within the game. I had also gone back to my original position, as inside-right, scoring five goals in one particular game – you never lose it! The standard at Frome Town, then, was better than at Peasedown, although I wasn't rubbing shoulders with the likes of Frank Blunstone any more. Army life had made me a more disciplined person and I felt the lads at Mortimers looked upon me as a man now, as opposed to a skinny apprentice. Ken was still there and life carried on largely as it had done before I'd been drafted. Meanwhile, my wage for playing the game I loved had risen. Frome Town were now paying me the princely sum of £2 a week!

However, an FA Cup defeat by Chippenham was about to change my direction once again. The loss of vital revenue meant that Frome couldn't afford to pay me the same money any longer and they asked if I'd accept half of the £2. Bloody hell, I thought, I've not even had time to enjoy my rise before it's gone, through no fault of my own. Ernie Marshall, the clerk of the works at Mortimers, who incidentally had played for Bath City, had always been interested in how my football career was progressing. When I showed him the letter Frome Town had sent me regarding the wage cut, he asked if he could take it and show the boss, Arthur Mortimer, who also happened to be chairman of Bath City. Mr Mortimer told me that Bath would pay the same wage I'd originally been on at Frome Town and, in January 1956, I agreed to join my home-town club, Bath City.

There'd be no need for a 45-minute journey to Badger's Hill any more – I could walk or cycle to Twerton Park from our house on Upper Bristol Road and my dad could save a small fortune in fuel costs. The boss at Bath was Bob Hewison, and when I met him for the first time he said, 'You're a young lad and you might have to wait your chance for first-team football,' which was fair enough. They actually put me on £4 a week – I'd doubled my money and at last felt that I was making genuine progress, though the money was only an added bonus and not a driving force for me.

My life now was bricklaying in the day, training with Bath on Tuesday and Thursday evenings, getting the bus to Peasedown to see Sylvia on Wednesday nights, and then playing on Saturdays for Bath. I was happy to be playing for the team that most of my family and friends supported and, now that I was earning two proper wages, I felt secure enough to ask Sylvia to be my wife. She accepted my marriage proposal, thankfully, and we were married in 1957.

Bath City were in the Southern League – not dissimilar to the Conference – and non-League football was particularly strong at that time, with a lot of players coming out from the Football League to play part-time and earn a living outside the game, too. Many of them doubled their income and some maybe earned even treble. At Bath, we had Ian Black, who had kept goal for Fulham. Charlie Fleming, who had been with Sunderland, was at Twerton Park, too, and even the great Stanley Mortensen from Blackpool. I was also playing against the likes of Tommy Lawton, who was with Kettering, and Wilf Mannion, of Middlesbrough. It was a great apprenticeship for me – and a bloody long one, too! I felt that if I was holding my own against players who had established themselves at the highest level of the game, maybe I had a chance of getting on myself. I had once again reverted to full-back after a year or so at Bath, filling in for an injured defender and I would, of course, remain there for the rest of my playing career.

We had several decent FA Cup runs whilst I was at the club but, without doubt, the best was when we reached the third round in January 1964. We'd seen off Maidenhead in the first round and then travelled to meet Wimbledon, who were the Amateur Cup-holders at that time. It was a difficult match for us but we came away with a 2–2 draw and had another crack at them at Twerton. The media were beginning to take notice of Bath by now and if we won, we'd be facing First Division Bolton in the next round. We hammered Wimbledon 4–0 to set up the biggest day in Bath City's history. A crowd of 12,800 packed in to see the type of game the FA Cup is all about and for a time, it looked like we might actually pull off a famous victory. Ken Owens put us ahead, but an unknown 17 year old called Francis Lee equalised six minutes later to earn Bolton a replay. Despite most of the neutrals in football willing us on, we lost 3–0 at Burnden Park, but the people of Bath still talk about that Cup run to this day.

I was now an established member of the Bath City team and, after about four years with the club, Nottingham Forest invited me up to play in an exhibition match so they could take a closer look at me. I travelled up to Nottingham with chairman Arthur Mortimer, his driver Ralph Powell and a lad called Brian Milsom, a wing-half at Bath who was basically invited to keep me company. We played in a charity match for the Forest Select side, against a team organised by Joe Mercer, who was Aston Villa's boss at the time. Milsom, who had just come along for the ride, had a hell of a game, and whether or not it was just a case of being in the right place at the right time, or the gods having a good laugh at my expense, I don't know. The upshot was – and you can probably see this coming – Milsom was snapped up by Forest, who decided not to follow up their interest in me. Bloody typical! He did OK for them, too. We kept in touch and I would see him occasionally when he came back home. It was back to Twerton Park for me, and I just kept my head down and carried on – what else could I do? I would certainly never have got anywhere if I'd gone around sulking and thinking what might have been. That's never been my style, and I wasn't going to start behaving that way then, but I'd be lying if I didn't admit that I felt the more chances passed me by, the less chance I had of succeeding at a higher level. Time was moving on, but I kept believing. I had to.

Back at Bath, the gates at Twerton averaged around 3,000 unless we had an FA Cup match against a League side. Ties against Exeter City, Brighton & Hove Albion and Bolton Wanderers would draw in crowds of up to 12,000. We had a good team spirit and three or four good FA Cup runs in my time there, but the battle with Bolton Wanderers is probably my most memorable. Around this time, I'd returned from injury after damaging my knee ligaments and my first game back was against Wisbech Town. They had a winger who used to play for Sunderland called Billy Elliott – and no, he didn't tiptoe around like a ballerina – and I hit him hard early on. He was one of the game's tougher characters and he got up from the tackle and said: 'Next time I'll break your fucking leg.' I've never sought protection from anybody on the pitch and I could always look out for myself, but on this occasion I turned to our strapping centre-half Ian McFarlane and said, 'Hey, big man, this fella's going to do me,' – but he never did. Maybe the thought of big Ian being on my side was enough to put him off.

The lads at Mortimers never held back on the Monday after the matches and comments of 'You were shite on Saturday', and suchlike, were not uncommon. I have to add, though, that they were equally fulsome with their praise. It was all good grounding, but starting work at 6 a.m. five days a week was enough to keep anyone's feet firmly on the ground. I'd been with Bath City for six seasons and was now captaining the side. At 28, I obviously believed my chances of playing League football had all but disappeared. I had every right to believe that if no club had come in for me after all this time, it was probably never going to happen. Then, someone entered my life and things would never be quite the same again. Long-serving Bath manager Bob Hewison was coming towards the end of his time in football. He'd been in the game for most of his life and he had seen enough. So, with old Bob moving on, for the start of the 1962–63 season Bath appointed Malcolm Allison as the new boss. Allison was a brash cockney lad who had played for West Ham but had been forced to quit the game when he had a collapsed lung removed. He'd been coaching at Cambridge University for a while and was considered a bright prospect by many in the game, and those in the know suggested his star would shine brightly in future years. Bath chairman Arthur Mortimer gave Allison his first big break and his arrival would eventually give me mine, too.

My introduction to Allison was somewhat odd, if only for the location. I was working on a site opposite Bath's Twerton Park home ground and was several stories up a new building. The chairman brought the new manager up to where I was working and said, 'Tony, this is the new manager of Bath City.' I shook hands with Malcolm and wished him all the best, but I couldn't help thinking what a flash sod he was in his expensive jacket complete with his swaggering, confident attitude. It wasn't hard to see how he'd impressed Arthur Mortimer, but I thought to myself that this fish was definitely too big for our pond. Things soon began to change, and training went from two nights a week to four nights a week. A lot of the lads thought it was asking a bit much of part-time professionals but once you got into the training you knew Malcolm was going to be top class. He began to bring in a few new players and, with the extra training and his additional one-on-one coaching with certain lads, including myself, he worked wonders for the team. We began to really fly in the League and, full of self-belief and team spirit, we won the Southern League for the first time in years in his first season as a manager. He always looked the part on the training ground. He had these big legs with shorts that he rolled up and tucked down and he was always smart. A few times after sessions he'd pull players to one side and tell them he wanted to do an extra twenty minutes one-on-one, if he felt there was something he could help improve. He showed an interest in me and undoubtedly helped to make me a better player. The whole place lit up in a short space of time and I would suggest only Malcolm Allison could have had that effect. One of the most unforgettable moments of Malcolm's time at Bath was when he asked me to meet a team of all-stars from around the London area who were playing at Bath in a charity game. He had so many connections throughout the game that the event itself was no real surprise: unlike the sight of the coach when it pulled up, however. I was expecting about 15 or so players to be on board, but as it drove into the bus station I could see it was absolutely packed, with lots of people standing in the aisles. I asked the first bloke to get off why there were so many players and he said: 'Half of them don't play, mate. They're bookmakers chasing Malcolm for what he owes them!' It summed Mal up perfectly!

Word of Allison's talents had spread over to North America and he was invited to coach in Canada for the summer. Before he flew out, he told me where he was headed and asked if I would like to join him as a guest for Toronto City. 'I'd like you to come over now but I can't fix it up at the moment,' he said to me. 'You'll have to wait for me to get sorted out and then I'll get you over.' I thought it probably wouldn't happen, and after a few weeks passed with no word I felt certain it wouldn't. Then, out of the blue, he sent a telegram to the building site I was working on, saying that he'd sorted it out and my plane tickets would be following shortly. I was to meet Johnny Brooks at Heathrow, who would also be playing for Toronto. Brooks was a Spurs player and, having never flown before, I was glad that I'd have some company. Sylvia was as understanding as ever and, despite it meaning we'd have virtually no time together over the summer, I was soon on my way to Canada. I made my way to Heathrow to meet Johnny Brooks but, when I met him on arrival, he told me he couldn't fly out because he hadn't got his visa organised. My apprehension returned as I prepared to make my first ever flight.

I sat on the plane and tried to keep my mind occupied, and soon we were in the air and over the ocean. I couldn't sleep, and after what seemed like an eternity we finally began to descend into New York where I was to catch a connecting flight to Canada. If I'd accidentally slipped into a comfort zone, I immediately shot out of it as all my fears of flying quickly returned. Flashes and deafening crashes began to rock the aircraft as we entered a huge electrical storm near to the airport. It was my worst nightmare. Thunder and lightning continued to batter the flimsy tin box with wings I happened to be trusting my life with, and I just sat frozen in terror. Oh, for my humble bike ride from our home to Twerton Park in light drizzle! Thankfully, and maybe due to my new-found religion, we made it through the storm and landed safely. Pretty soon, we were once again airborne and I was on my way to Canada but, owing to this first experience, I can honestly say I've never been a good air traveller since.

Malcolm met me at the airport and I officially began my summer with Toronto City. I went to this hotel in Toronto where all the other lads were staying and we soon got to know each other well and enjoyed the company, while our families stayed behind in various countries around the globe. I enjoyed the Canadian way of life: the people, the food, the climate and the scenery. With most of the games being in mid-week there was one occasion when we all went deep into the woods for a weekend to stay in log cabins. I didn't venture out that much, with it being confirmed bear country, but it was a good experience.

I had become a full-time pro in Canada and was training during the day, and this was when things really began to happen for me. I was up against quality players from around the world and I think it was around this time that Malcolm fully decided that I was a useful player. My debut was against Italian side AS Roma and I was faced with the task of stopping their Brazilian winger, Peoti, who had been Pelé's club partner at Santos. Everything I did that day seemed to come off and Peoti didn't get a kick. Our goalkeeper, Aston Villa's Nigel Sims, said I was the best full-back he'd ever played behind. I'd played in front of 12,000 Italians that day and we'd come out on top. As I walked off the pitch, Malcolm said to me, 'You'll do.' That throwaway remark would prove to have a great impact on my career in the years to come.

Maybe Malcolm had just wanted a closer look in different settings. He'd never tell you that, but it was a possibility, especially if I was something of a puzzle to him. The North American sun was on my back and I was enjoying myself more than ever before. I even made it into a Canadian All-Stars side and we had a good tussle with Hearts who were on tour at the time. I was well into my three-month stint when Malcolm unexpectedly flew back to England. He'd got an interview for the vacant post at Plymouth Argyle and, hardly surprisingly, was successful in his application. He'd left a lasting impression at Bath City and everybody knew he was on his way to bigger and better things. Nobody begrudged him his move up the ladder, sad though it was to lose such a talent.

Bath City gave me permission to stay on in Toronto for a couple of weeks later than planned, and I returned home feeling fitter and stronger than ever. The Canadian experience had been just the boost I'd needed and, even though I was now 29 years old, it restored my self-belief that great things were still possible. I owed that confident feeling to Malcolm Allison. I'd also left Canada with the plaudit of being named the best full-back in the country, which again was a huge confidence-booster, considering I was still playing my English football in the Southern League. I reckoned if nothing happened on the back of this summer, it never would. I took a short holiday with Sylvia and then it was back down to business with Bath City. Meanwhile, Ivor Powell had taken over as boss at Twerton Park. He was a former Welsh international who'd been out at Bogota in South America and was a likeable bloke. He'd not been there long when he made a signing that grabbed the headlines in the *Bath Chronicle*. It read something like, 'Bath Sign Racing Club De Paris Star' – well worth the front page of any local paper . . . but all was not as it seemed. The truth about our international signing came out when we were travelling to a pre-season friendly match with Barry Town in South Wales. The coach journey became torturous after we became stranded on an A-road behind a high-loader that we couldn't overtake for love nor money. As we approached this tiny village in the middle of nowhere, this 'French' lad walked up to the front of the coach to talk to the driver. He'd hardly said boo to a goose since his arrival but he leaned over the driver's shoulder and said, 'Take a right here, mate.' A bit further on, he told the driver to make a left, and a minute or so later we were back on the road we'd been on previously. The high-loader was still there, only now it was behind us! He quietly went back to his seat as the rest of the coach sat in stunned silence. This so-called star from Paris had actually been making his living with a Welsh League side and the whole thing had been made up for sensationalism. Needless to say, it caused much mirth amongst the lads and we welcomed the new guy perhaps even more warmly than before.

I was having a great pre-season with Bath and, part-way through, Plymouth Argyle came in with an offer to buy me. It was a little hard to believe that, after all these years, I was going to play for a Second Division professional football club. To my despair, though, my club turned Argyle down! All these years of working towards a break and Bath knocked it back! I had to go to the manager and plead my case. Hadn't I given them years of loyal service? Didn't they owe me at least a crack at fulfilling my dream? I was now coming up to my 30th birthday and this was most likely my last chance. To their eternal credit, they considered my case and agreed to accept a fee of £1,500 from Argyle. There was one final problem to overcome. Malcolm told me he wouldn't be able to get the board to sanction a deal for a 30-year-old defender with no League experience so he told me to make a slight amendment to my birth certificate. I dug it out and looked at the creased old document. One of the folds happened to cross my date of birth. With careful alteration, I was able to tack two years on to my real birth date, which changed from 1934 to 1936, and, hey presto, I was two years younger! That piece of skulduggery was, believe it or not, enough to seal the deal. The Plymouth board were happy enough with a 28-year-old player, and so I signed my first professional contract. I'd made it into League football at last and all the patience, hard work and persistence had paid off. I left Bath having never been dropped in 8 years and having made more than 400 appearances for them. Whatever happened from here on in, I would never forget my time at Twerton Park. One thing I did regret was that Sylvia's dad, Wyndum Mitchard, never saw me make the grade in League football. He took such a great interest in my career and loved following Bath City. He would have loved the fact that I'd finally broken into League football, but he died shortly before my move to Plymouth. My brother-in-law, Eric Doughty, had been at Arsenal, and Wyndum supported him in the same way he had me. But poor Eric stayed at Highbury for ten years and played just one first-team match! He then transferred to Plymouth in 1961 and did his cruciate ligament in during his first League game for them. Eric's luck was well and truly out.

I kept the memory of Wyndum with me as I travelled to Plymouth, where Malcolm had once again shown faith in me. It was down to me now to repay him out on the pitch. I owed it to both him and myself to make the most of this opportunity.

FOUR

The Pilgrims and a Case of the Summertime Blues

'Tony Book is nearly 32 and, logically speaking, he has not got much longer to go in football. He may last six seasons but should he have an injury with us next season, I am sure we would never have got this kind of offer again.'

Derek Ufton, Plymouth Argyle manager (24 July 1966)

My first year at Plymouth saw my wages rise to £30 a week, plus bits and pieces in bonuses. I'd put the tools away and left bricklaying behind for now, but I was never sure how long my career would last, so I knew that, whatever happened, I had a good trade behind me if ever I needed it. We moved into a rented clubhouse, which was a swish three-bedroomed detached in the Plymouth suburbs, and left Somerset and our little terraced house behind to start a new life in Devon. There would be no getting up at 6 a.m. and taking a bus to our paid jobs – at least for a while – and we began to enjoy the trappings of playing for a League club. The full-time training, just as it had done in Canada, suited me down to the ground and I felt in tip-top shape for my first season as a professional. Malcolm used to take us training at the local naval base and several other venues to vary the training schedule as much as he could. We'd do gym work, go swimming, work with weights, or whatever he felt would benefit the squad and perhaps give us the slight edge over other teams. His coaching methods also included psychology, of which he was a master.

He'd be building you up and making you believe you could do anything, but every now and then he'd throw in a veiled threat. I could be sitting in the bath and the reserve full-back could be near by and Malcolm would say, 'I hear you're playing well at the moment. It won't be long before you're given a chance.' It was just a reminder – a subtle one at that – for me or any of the other lads it could apply to, that we had to keep on our toes – or else. He was also keen on one-on-one training when the main session had ended, and would take you to one side for fifteen minutes or so and practise things he felt could improve your game. I knew him well by this time from our time together at Bath and in Canada, so I appreciated his methods and they weren't strange to me. Some days he'd have you back for afternoon training as well as the regular morning session, which was pretty unique in those days.

I was determined to make the most of my late start in professional football and was giving everything I had in pre-season. It paid off, too, as Malcolm put me straight into the first team as vice captain and things went well for both the side and myself. Argyle were a decent Second Division team with a huge fan base – they would often get gates of more than 25,000 – and we progressed to the semi-finals of the 1964–65 League Cup where we lost over two legs to Leicester City. By the end of the season I'd played in every game and enjoyed it immensely. The team had finished in the top six and I didn't feel out of my depth at all, and life at Home Park couldn't have been better.

I even went into business with teammate Johnny Newman, the club skipper, opening a florist's. It was called The Mannamead Flower Box. It was a lovely part of the world to live in, but right off the map, football-wise. We used to leave on a Friday for every away trip, either by train or coach, and if we were playing a game in the north-east it would be Sunday morning before we arrived home. Most return journeys meant connecting at London, spending a few hours there and catching the sleeper train back to Plymouth. On the pitch, Malcolm had started bringing a few kids through into the first team: lads like Norman Piper, Richard Reynolds and Michael Trebilcock, who all did well. Mike would eventually sign for First Division Everton. With the likes of Newman, Frank Lord and myself also in the team, there was a good mix and a great team spirit.

During my first year in Devon, Sylvia gave birth to our first child, a little girl, who we named Tracey. It was perfect timing in many ways, because now that I was immersed in the professional footballer's way of life I was spending less and less time at home. My wife never complained about my absence because she knew that I was fulfilling a dream and, as ever, she just let me get on with things and, thankfully, her mother Beatrice stayed with us for a while to help out. Our daughter would mean that Sylvia, who wasn't working for the first time in her life since our move south, wouldn't feel lonely whilst I was on long trips to Middlesbrough and Sunderland – she wouldn't have the time! I'm afraid I wasn't present at the birth. I'm far too squeamish for things like that and I wouldn't have been comfortable with the whole birth procedure. I went along when it was all over, having waited at home until I was given the all clear! I can feel the disapproval of a thousand women even now!

I was still pinching myself that the past 12 months had been real, but I had no idea how long it would all last. That thought drove me on even harder and I trained and played like a man possessed, in the knowledge that the clock was ticking and time was against me. If Plymouth Argyle was to be the pinnacle of my career, I was certainly going to give it my best shot and make an impression while I had the chance. I kept hearing the officials at Bath saying it probably wouldn't be long before I was back playing for them because of my age and again, it spurred me on to think of myself more as a player in his early 20s than a player approaching his 31st birthday. It was all new to me and perhaps this was to be the key to my longevity as a player.

Malcolm Allison was the same wherever he was, whether it was in London, Bath or Plymouth. He was enjoying the champagne lifestyle, which suited him perfectly, and if you ever met him whilst out socialising he'd have you over to his table and the champagne bottles would be flowing as he held court. We were from different worlds, and if you took away the football we would never have spoken or worked together in our lives. I was never close to him at all, despite the respect I had for him; it was just the way things were. I've never been the best of drinkers, even though I enjoy a pint now and then, and I certainly couldn't have kept up with Malcolm or lived his fast-lane lifestyle. If I had, I wouldn't have lasted five minutes. Yet he was a generous man who did care about people, as I had discovered during my days at Bath.

In 1962, Sylvia had had a miscarriage, and obviously we were both upset and felt incredibly empty. I bumped into Malcolm a few days after and he said, 'Come on, you're coming with me.' I didn't really feel like going, but he was insistent, so I went along. He took me from Bath down to Bristol to a club near the television studios and bought me drinks all evening. We set off home in his big old battered car and I was sitting in the back choking on his cigar smoke. Hardly surprising that I was sick out of the window and rough for two days afterwards. It may have been unorthodox, but it was his way of dealing with things. He just wanted to take my mind off our loss for a few hours and I appreciated the gesture, if not the immediate after-effects.

Malcolm's main haunt in Plymouth was the Ace of Clubs, and he wouldn't mind if the whole team had drunk the night away as long as they were doing the business on the pitch – an attitude I believe most football fans would agree with. He enjoyed a good time and wanted the players to enjoy themselves, too. Back in his days at Bath he would often tell the coach driver on the way back from a Southern League away match to pull in at the next pub he came to, and we could be there for the rest of the night. It was his way, and nobody could argue that it didn't get results, and if he had money in his pocket he would have to spend it, and the players loved him for it. They would have run through rings of fire for him because he treated them like adults, and they responded accordingly. People either loved him or hated him – there wasn't too much middle ground with Malcolm Allison. Our visits to London were rarely dull and he was always taking us to some new club or other. A few drinks certainly helped everyone sleep on the journey back to Devon.

He had many friends in the capital and was always introducing them to us, but his regular pals were the ex-Arsenal players Arthur Shaw and Jimmy Logie. All the champagne days at Home Park, however, were about to end. During the close season, Manchester City's new manager, Joe Mercer, approached Malcolm to be his coach at Maine Road. He left for an interview and, before we knew it, his bags were packed and he was off to the bright lights of Manchester. Again, nobody begrudged him the move, and even though City were in the same division as Plymouth at the time, everyone knew that Malcolm and his new club were both destined for great things. I was just grateful that he'd given me the chance to make my way at professional level. I thought it was the end of our working relationship and, for the next 12 months, it was exactly that.

Derek Ufton, Malcolm's assistant at Home Park, took over and things ticked along fairly well. (At this point, incidentally, Malcolm told him that I was in fact nearly 32, not nearly 30, and no fuss was made.) Argyle, however, were never going to be more than they already were. During the 1965–66 season, City travelled down to Plymouth for a League match that they would lose 1–0, and they stayed over in a Torquay hotel. Mike Summerbee (or Buzzer, as he was popularly known) was now at Maine Road, and I knew him from my days at Bath where we had come up against each other a few times. He asked me to come and have a drink with him after the match, which I did. I'd had no connection with City at that point and, while there was talk of a few other clubs showing an interest in me, there were no firm offers. I read things in the paper, such as Leicester City were apparently preparing a bid of something like £20,000, but I just concentrated on doing my best at Plymouth. Then there was reported interest from Manchester City, but again there were no firm offers. I would be lying if I said that the paper talk didn't excite me at the time. It wasn't so long ago that I'd been laying bricks for a living and playing part-time football for Bath City, and now one of the most famous clubs in England was believed to be considering a bid for my services.

Manchester City were crowned champions of Division Two at the end of that season, and they'd impressed me when Plymouth played at Maine Road and earned a 1–1 draw. Maine Road was an intimidating ground, and City had plenty of talent in their side, such as Glyn Pardoe, Johnny Crossan and Neil Young. There was something tangible in the electrically charged Moss Side air. You could tell they were going places.

During the close season of 1966, after I'd completed my second year at Home Park, I was made officially aware that the interest from newly promoted City was firm. The stumbling block would be Malcolm convincing Joe Mercer to sign a 31-year-old full-back with just two years' experience as a professional. I'd later discover City had considered almost every full-back around but they couldn't make their minds up. By all accounts, it was a chance remark from Malcolm about signing me that set the deal in motion. Joe commented that I was 31 years old, and Mal countered, 'How old were you, Joe, when you left Everton to go to Arsenal?' Joe replied he was 31 and Mal had proved his point with a simple question. He had also cleared the path for me to become a Manchester City player.

City made an offer but, just as had happened at Bath City,

Plymouth turned down their initial bid. In fact, Argyle demanded what was then a staggering £35,000! Once again, I had to go cap in hand to the manager, pleading for them to let me go because the opportunity represented everything that I had ever wanted to do. I desperately wanted to test myself by playing at the highest level and this had to be the final chance of doing so. Eventually, they accepted a bid of £17,500 – exactly half their original asking price – and I was at last on my way to Maine Road. If somebody had said to me whilst I was playing in the Southern League for Bath that I could have one good season with Manchester City I would have been more than happy with my lot. But even in my wildest dreams I couldn't have imagined what was in store for me with the Blues.

Summer 1966 was the first time I met Joe Mercer to discuss my move to City. He'd invited me to England's World Cup match against Argentina and, after linking up with him in London, we headed for the underground. There was another bloke coming along with us, who we met on the tube, but I had no idea who he was. Joe introduced me to the man – Frank Clough – who it turned out was one of the leading football reporters of the time. Joe didn't want Frank to know I was about to join City and, as he obviously didn't know me at the time anyway, Joe said, 'This is my friend John Smith from Plymouth,' and added that I was just going along to the game with them. A few weeks later, after I'd put pen to paper on the deal, Frank came up to me and said, 'How I didn't cop on to that deal I'll never know!'

I watched the England game with Joe and had a chat with him later, and everything was agreed. He told me there was no money in the well, and that, despite what people might have thought at the time, considering I was leaving Plymouth for Manchester City, he'd only be able to up my money from £35 to £40 a week. I told Joe that would do me fine – I'd come this far and wasn't about to let a few quid get in the way of things. Joe wasn't a well man at the time but he was a lovely bloke and I desperately wanted to play for him. He and Malcolm took me to another World Cup match, this time at Everton, and I signed shortly afterwards. Joe told me that they'd give me a one-year contract with a one-year option. I asked him what the option was and he said, 'If you don't do the business you'll be back down to the West Country at the end of the season!' So I knew I had to go and play and show everyone what I could do or I'd be out. That's how it was back then.

I was now a City player and as I watched the World Cup final a few weeks later it really hit home that I'd finally cracked it. England had beaten West Germany at Wembley and the lads that were now wearing World Cup-winners' medals would be the same ones I'd be up against week in, week out in the colours of Manchester City. It was an amazing summer for me, and one that I will never forget.

FIVE

City Life and the Kray Twins

'You look fit enough, son. You look like I used to. There's
nothing of you – you look really well.'

Joe Mercer, July 1966

The question I kept asking myself, as pre-season training
approached, was whether or not I could hold my own at First
Division level. I'd done well at Plymouth, but this was another step
up again. Even though I felt as fit as I'd ever done, I couldn't know
how things would go until the season had actually started. We had
no house sorted as yet in the Manchester area so I became a
temporary resident at the Grand Hotel on Aytoun Street in
Manchester city centre. I'd go to training, come back around four
o'clock, have a cup of tea in the lounge, read a book and try to
relax as best I could. I wasn't what you'd exactly call a hell-raiser!
Sylvia was still in Plymouth with our daughter because we didn't
want to unsettle her by constantly changing her surroundings and
hotel life is not ideal for any child, so I was a bit lonely for those
first few weeks in Manchester.

In fact, being a quiet West Country lad, I think a few of the
locals began to think I was a bit of an oddball. There was a bar

opposite the hotel called the Piccadilly Club and I used to pop over about nine o'clock and have a couple of beers and then go back to the hotel. Malcolm had introduced me to the owners but I don't think they could ever quite understand why a professional footballer only stayed for a couple and then left before it became lively. I suppose it just wasn't the done thing, especially in swinging '60s Manchester, which was a million miles away from what I was used to. They were probably used to the likes of Mike Summerbee and George Best painting the town red, so perhaps I was a bit of a conundrum to them.

When the lads who ran the Piccadilly Club saw Malcolm, they asked him, 'Is Tony all right?' Mal asked them what they meant, and they said they couldn't understand why I left so early, when things were just beginning to liven up. I imagine that Malcolm said little but probably had a wry smile on his face. I was so into being a professional footballer that I was desperate to behave in public as I believed I should and, in doing so, perhaps I forgot to let my hair down once in a while. I suppose I was just a bit green at the time.

Malcolm was still a rum bugger and I remember one particular time when he took us to this casino in Manchester. Mal had his eye on one of the girls who worked there. I think she was a croupier, or something like that, and he was flirting with her all night. When she'd finished her shift, he asked her if he could come around and stay at her house. 'No,' she replied. 'Besides, I only have a single bed.' It would take more than that to shake off Mal, though. After he'd found out where she lived, he went to Kendal's and bought a double bed, which he had sent to her address. I've no idea what happened after that, but it gives an indication of just how irrepressible he was. At the end of the day, he was a loveable rogue more than anything else.

On the football side of things, I was glad to hear Joe was becoming stronger all the time and really getting his health back. He'd suffered badly whilst at Aston Villa and I know the doctors had advised him against taking a managerial job again until he'd fully recovered. So what did he do? He took on the most stressful job in football! Malcolm was in charge of all the training and Joe took care of the public relations side of managing the Blues – no mean feat when you consider the size of the club. You just knew this partnership had a real chance of becoming something special because the two of them had the perfect balance. Joe was always dressed in a suit and stayed away from the coaching side of things, while Malcolm's place was out on the training pitch. That's how they worked. Joe left Malcolm to get on with things, and Malcolm appreciated being able to work without restraints. That's how you got the best out of Malcolm, and Joe knew it. As the new boy at Maine Road, I found the players very welcoming towards me, and I was perhaps fortunate that I knew Mike Summerbee from our West Country days. In fact, the first time we played against each other I believe we squared up to one another! It was just our competitiveness and nothing more, and knowing Mike definitely helped me settle in.

Mike was close to the captain, Johnny Crossan, and in my early days at City I socialised a lot with those two lads. Mike was single at the time and was a man about town, enjoying the bachelor life to the full with his mate Besty, but Johnny was married with two young kids and often we'd go back to his house and enjoy the afternoon with his family. Johnny was sharp as a tack and great company to be around and Buzzer was never short of a witty line or two. I remember Johnny once reading something a reporter had written about him and then destroying the poor chap the next time they met with a few carefully chosen words. I'll not reveal exactly what he said but the reporter was left blushing, and no doubt wishing he'd become a milkman or something.

Sylvia had been up to Manchester a few times to look for a home and, midway through the season, we decided to move into one of the club's houses in Sale. We soon discovered our neighbours on either side were Manchester United fans. They were a friendly bunch, though, and once we'd got to know them we felt completely at home.

This all happened after I'd made my debut for City, so I'd best backtrack a little. My first game was away to Southampton, and it gave me my first experience of the wind-up merchants that were my new teammates. Although we'd lost 1–0, I'd had a decent enough game, and back then the *Manchester Evening News* used to have an award called 'Monday's Man', which went to the outstanding performer of the weekend's matches. Peter Gardner was the reporter for City at the time, and Crossan and Buzzer told me that Gardner had told them I was going to be Monday's Man and that I would get a cheque for £500 – the standard payment for the award . . . or so they said. I was made up, and spent the journey home thinking about ways to spend it. I needn't have bothered. It later transpired that I was indeed Monday's Man, but the money was nowhere to be seen. I said to Buzzer at training on the following Tuesday, 'When do I get my £500?' and he just laughed and told me they'd been pulling my leg. The lousy beggars! The only prize was the honour of winning the award! Oh well, I wised up pretty quickly after that.

My home debut was against Liverpool and it felt fantastic to be playing in front of a packed Maine Road – 50,320 people were there that day to watch a game of football. This was what it was all about, and this was the reason I'd worked hard for so long. The City fans made me feel welcome and I think they could see that I was trying my best to help their side win. I think if you do that, wherever you are, supporters will always get behind you, especially City fans, who love nothing more than a wholehearted player. The beauty of the side I was playing in was the number of young local lads that were in the first team. There was Glyn Pardoe, Alan Oakes, Mike Doyle and Neil Young, who were all at the right age to take the next step forward after winning promotion. They also knew what it meant to play for Manchester City, as most of them had supported the club as kids and stood on the terraces with their dads.

My instructions from the management were to go out and use

my experience on the pitch and to play to my strengths. Having played against some of the top players in the country during my time at Bath (the stars who had joined non-League clubs and taken on another job as well), my experience held me in fairly good stead. From time to time I was used as a sweeper – a position which Malcolm had also employed at Plymouth. I remember that the first time I played in this position was in a League match for Argyle at Bury. Malcolm had switched around the tactics and we beat Bury, but we had to face them again in the League Cup a few days later. They must have thought we wouldn't try the same tactics so soon after, but we did, and we won again. This made Mal pretty confident about me playing there again if the situation demanded it, and boded well for City's main aim in the First Division, which was to consolidate our position and establish ourselves as a worthy team.

Back at the Grand Hotel I witnessed a dramatic event that certainly livened up my sleepy afternoon routine. I arrived back after training as normal and sat down in the lounge for a cup of tea. The manager from the Piccadilly Club, who knew I was a City player, was in there too, and he came over and said he would like to introduce me to a couple of his friends from London. Before I'd got to their table, though, the police appeared from everywhere. I turned around and discreetly left the lounge, wondering what it was all about. Later, I was told that the friends were Ronnie and Reggie Kray, who had come to Manchester on 'business'. I didn't know them from Adam to look at, but was aware of their reputation – perhaps it was a good thing the police came when they did!

I would meet Britain's most notorious criminals again, not that long after that incident, and it was no less dramatic than the first time. The team and I were going to go to Brighton for a break but we stopped over in London after a game. We went into a club that Malcolm had recommended and were having a great time. One of the lads was winking at a girl on another table. When this lad went to the toilet, a bloke, who'd been sitting at the same table as the girl, followed him in. Once in there, he turned nasty, threatening our lad and telling him that if there was any nonsense, he'd have his kneecaps blown off. Looking a bit unnerved, he came back to the table and told Malcolm about it. It turned out that the Kray twins were in the club, and Mal went straight over to their table. He bent over and told them what had gone on. Moments later, Ronnie and Reggie Kray went over to this bloke and had a quiet word in his ear. Within a few minutes, he left the club looking a bit ashen-faced, having obviously been told he'd just threatened to hurt one of the Kray twins' personal friends. I can only guess at exactly what they said, but it proved that Malcolm was a handy lad to know and had certainly made some, shall we say, interesting connections over the years.

Not long after that, on our return home, the same player that had almost caused an outbreak of East End-style gangland violence asked me if I needed anything for the house. I said I was sure my wife would find a use for anything I brought home and he told me to park my car at the back of a well-known department store in the middle of Manchester. I did just that and left the car keys with the store man and then went for a coffee. After a little wander around the town centre, I came back, collected my keys and drove home and tentatively took a look in the boot. When I opened it I found a big box of china crockery! I decided it was probably best not to repeat the trip to town, so when I was asked next time I politely declined.

Back on the pitch, my first season with the Blues was going well, and we were sticking to our aim of consolidating our position. Nobody expected us to be challenging for the title but, by the same token, our fans would have been horrified if we had gone straight back to Division Two. We were terribly inconsistent and, even back in the 1960s, it was invariably a case of 'which City has turned up today?' – nothing much has changed over the years, has it? I felt Joe and Malcolm were happy to go along with that whilst looking at ways to improve things for the future. This didn't necessarily mean new players arriving – they seemed fairly happy with what they'd got – but more focus on new training methods and ways to get the best out of their squad. They would add new faces, but only a couple here and there, and the signings would always be top class and would fit in with the team almost from the word go. The injection of new blood was always perfectly timed and they never seemed to waste a penny of the club's money.

My first derby game was at Old Trafford. It was an intense occasion for me, personally, as I was thrust into the biggest derby match in England. It was my first real experience of what the fixture actually meant to the City fans, though, of course, I already had a fair idea of what it was all about. There was a tremendous buzz about the place on the build-up to the match and there was a frantic clamour for tickets. With me only just arriving I had no need for my allocation and was happy to give my spare tickets to Mike Doyle, Alan Oakes or Glyn Pardoe – the local lads who had many family members and friends desperate to get to the match. The nearest I'd come to the Manchester derby was playing for Plymouth against Bristol City, so it was difficult to take in the atmosphere of the game, which, incidentally, United won 1–0 in front of the biggest crowd I'd ever played before at that point – 62,500. I was up against George Best in what was to be the first of many tussles with the talented Irishman and I think I did OK.

In future years he would pay me the compliment of saying I was one of his most difficult opponents, which I consider to be high praise indeed. I suppose it was my pace that enabled me to keep up with him, but he was a tricky so-and-so. In my opinion, he was the best player I ever came up against, because he could do everything. Denis Law was lethal in the box and Bobby Charlton could distribute fantastic balls all over the park but George Best could do the lot. I used to run alongside the little beggar, trying to get him off the ball. I'd say, 'Pass the ball, you bugger, pass it!' knowing that the threat would ease once he'd released it. He'd laugh at my suggestions, and we'd both have our work cut out. We had our scraps, then, but Besty knew I always stuck to my task, which I think is why he spoke so highly of me. He was a genuine kid on the field and I had a lot of time for him.

During our tussles, meanwhile, we could both hear the United coaches on the touchline urging him to 'take the old bugger on!' I loved it when that happened, because it was a challenge for me to show what I was capable of. Tommy Kavanagh, the assistant boss at Old Trafford, used to try to wind me up by telling anyone who was taking me on to 'run the old bastard!' I'd pass him and give him a mouthful back because I wouldn't take anything lying down as a player. In fact, you could say that, as a player, I was a big shit! I'd go back to Kavanagh, who was there with his silvery hair, mouthing off as usual, and I'd shout, 'You're a bit of an old bastard yourself!' I would mellow when I became a manager, but as a player it was totally different.

As far as my own teammates went, I was slowly getting to know them all fairly well. Our goalkeeper, Harry Dowd, had been in the building trade and was one of those blokes who never worried about anything. You might have a match with somebody like West Ham at the weekend and you could speak to Harry on the morning of the game and he wouldn't have a clue as to which team we were playing! He just went out and did his job and wasn't interested in anything else. It was actually a nice attitude to have, because nothing ever fazed him and he never suffered from nerves. In fact, if any of the lads had butterflies before a big match and needed a leveller, all they needed to do was glance over to Harry, who looked as if he was waiting for the No. 25 bus. One of the best games I ever saw him have was during a friendly in Belgium. It was an end-of-season tour and we all treated it as a holiday, because that's the way Malcolm wanted it. The night before we played Standard Liege, Harry was drunk as a lord. You'd have put money on him feeling like crap the next day, but he was absolutely brilliant. He kept a clean sheet and even saved a penalty – but that was Harry: an amazing character. He was a good shot-stopper and a very good goalkeeper who did well for us, as did Ken Mulhearn, who was sharing first team responsibilities for a while.

Glyn Pardoe, or 'Solly' as we called him, because of his likeness to some Arab bloke in a film of the time, was a lad I rated very highly. As a right-footed full-back playing on the left side you needed something a bit extra – not only to play there but to play there well, which Glyn did. Alongside him was his cousin, Alan Oakes, and they made a great team on the left side of the pitch. George Heslop was a solid defender who was famed for his wraparound haircut. I didn't even realise that he was bald underneath that comb-over for a long while – like I said, I was a bit green back then! Mike Doyle was a local lad and a City fan through and through, and he loved the derby games more than anyone. Let me confirm at this point that he really did hate United with a passion. It certainly wasn't an act! Mike hung around with Glyn, Oakey and Colin Bell, and Doyley was definitely the leader. He was always organising things (golf days, drinking sessions and suchlike) – a bit like he was on the pitch. He was a solid and dependable half-back who should have won far more England caps than he actually did.

Alan Oakes was a quiet lad with a dry sense of humour and another player – and man – you could depend on week in, week out. Stan Horne, who was I believe the first black lad to represent the club, was on the fringe of the side but would do a solid job when required. Stan was a popular lad with an easy-going nature and was unlucky to have players of such high calibre ahead of him because he was a good player himself. He had followed Joe Mercer from Aston Villa but suffered from high blood pressure, according to the doctors. That finished him at Villa, but Stan, a good-looking, sharp-dressed fellow, wouldn't accept anything was wrong because he felt fine. He had further tests that showed he was fit and able to play so he wrote to Joe and was granted a trial at City. Joe probably thought that, as he himself had been given another chance to get on with what he loved, why not give Stan the same opportunity? Stan passed his medical at Maine Road and did a sterling job whenever he played.

As I said, I knew Buzzer before I came to Maine Road, so I knew what a character he was. Whenever anything was going down on or off the pitch he'd be close by. He was a West Country lad who had come to a big city and was enjoying himself immensely. He was a good mate of George Best and it would be hard to think of a livelier pair on the town. On the pitch, all I had to do was feed the ball to Buzzer's feet and he would do the rest, and there weren't too many defenders who could match him. He was a tremendous talent, who gave his very best years to Manchester City and was as important as any member of the squad. His on-field antics occasionally had us all in stitches but he was nobody's fool and never gave less than total commitment every time he played for the club. One thing he used to do, egged on by Malcolm, was about an hour before the kick-off of an Old Trafford Manchester derby, go down towards the Stretford End and wave to the United fans. When he got close to the corner flag, he'd pretend to wipe his nose on it and the Reds always took the bait. On the pitch, he'd give out the odd snarl if someone was getting on his nerves, but if he felt the referee was taking it all too seriously, he'd find some way of lightening the mood by doing something daft. One time he took the linesman's flag and ran up and down the touchline for a few seconds – the crowd loved him for it but he'd probably get sent off about a dozen times a season in today's humourless game.

Colin Bell was the king to the City fans and commanded total respect from his teammates and fellow professionals. He was a special talent and back then there was no better box-to-box player in the country. He had an engine that ran smoother than a Rolls-Royce and was the beating heart of the team when we were flying. He was a quiet, unassuming lad who had it all. Johnny Crossan was another great midfielder, who I had a lot to thank for socially, as well as on the pitch. He was a great player with tremendous technical ability garnered from his experiences at Standard Liege and Sparta Rotterdam. Whilst he may have been one of the most amiable blokes you could ever meet, he could look after himself on the football field and was always the first to back you up if there was any trouble brewing. Dave Connor, or 'Tadger' as we all used to call him, for reasons I won't reveal, was a great utility player who was often given specific jobs by Malcolm. He'd be asked to snuff out players on a man-to-man marking basis and whoever he was playing against used to hate it because he was so effective at his job. He'd stick to them like a limpet and, though he wasn't a star-name, he won us many games by marking the opposition's main threat out of the game. Neil Young had a swagger to his game and was an elegant forward who could glide past opponents with almost embarrassing ease. Give Nelly a chance in the box and you could put a fair amount of money on the ball ending up in the back of the net.

All over the pitch we had players who complemented each other, and that would prove to be one of the secrets of our future success. We had a team spirit and belief that only comes around every now and then, and we had confidence instilled in us by Malcolm and Joe. I got to know the lads by mixing as much as I could with them on away trips. I always made a mental note of who I'd been sitting with or eating with the previous week and made sure it was someone different for our next match on the road. Maybe my background as captain of Plymouth Argyle or Bath City had made me this way, but it was something I wanted to do. I used to room with Buzzer, but because I was a quiet bloke who preferred a pint to a glass of champagne I hardly saw him after the match. If we went to London, he'd be gone most of the time, but I was happy with that – we were friends, but different people, and whilst he enjoyed the champagne lifestyle I invariably got my head down! I suppose I was a bit older than Mike, but I was married and he was single, and there's a world of difference.

Things couldn't have been going better at the club, and Sylvia and Tracey had moved into our new house in Sale, so I felt happier than I'd ever been as a player. I was settled and enjoying life in Manchester, which, though completely different from Bath and Plymouth, was still a homely and welcoming place in its own way.

Around December of 1966, I was even given the chance to return to my home town for a testimonial. City beat Bath City 5–0, but it was great to be back on my old stomping ground in front of the people who I used to play for week in, week out. The Twerton fans were great and gave me a great reception – a few of them possibly might have thought I'd be returning from Plymouth around about this time but they seemed happy that my career had gone beyond anyone's expectations, including my own. In fact, a few had even started a campaign in the local paper to have me honoured in some way for my move to City. It was good to have all my family watching, too, and it brought it all home to me how far I'd come since my days at Twerton Park.

In March 1967, my first and only son, Anthony, was born. He was the first Mancunian in the Book family, and if you cut him open today, he'd be blue inside. I'm afraid I ducked out of the birth again because my squeamish nature would probably have added to the nurse's problems had I been there. I dropped Sylvia off at the labour ward and headed for Platt Lane. During training, I got a call to say she'd had a baby boy. He arrived on time and they were both doing well. We now had a boy and a girl, and it made our family complete. I never pushed Anthony into football as time went on, and he was always a lad who seemed to shy away from any attention I ever received. If I went to the village and some kids spotted me and ran up for an autograph, he'd shy away from it, probably wondering why his dad was noticed and asked to do things other dads weren't. He's always loved the game but he never really played that much. He'd kick a ball around but never showed any interest in playing professionally. Both he and Tracey are City daft, though, and they follow them all over the place.

In April 1967, City progressed to the FA Cup quarter-final,

where we drew Leeds United away. We had been playing the sweeper system before we went into the tie but on the day we were told we would be changing to a 4–4–2 formation, and I believe it was around this time that we really began to take off as a team. We were desperately unlucky to lose that day, with the only goal of the game coming when Jackie Charlton headed home from a corner late on. This was the only time they'd hurt us in the entire game. We had missed many chances and ended up paying the price but the performance had convinced Joe and Malcolm to ditch the sweeper system and stick with the new plan. It seemed to suit the attacking instincts of the team perfectly.

There was to be another attacking change to our style, too, instigated by Mike Summerbee and Francis Lee. These two forwards were always coming in for rough treatment from opposing defenders, and I remember them saying after one game, 'It's about bleeding time us forwards starting tackling back and giving the defenders some of their own medicine.' It seemed an innocuous thing to say, and perhaps an obvious one, but it was an idea that was worth putting into practice. The forwards agreed that instead of just taking the ball past defenders, they would actively go looking for it when the defenders were in possession, and then make full-blooded challenges on them. From then on, Buzzer, Franny and whoever else was up front, would leave the odd ball so they could make a crunching challenge on the defender, and it began to work wonders. It added a new aggressive dimension to our attack that few, if any, other teams had.

Towards the end of this season, Tony Coleman arrived from Doncaster with a reputation for being a bit of a loose cannon – and it was a well-earned reputation, too. He was a scallywag scouser who, while playing for Bangor City, had punched a referee and consequently been banned for a while, but the fans and players took to him almost straight away and he looked right at home pretty much from the off. Malcolm had arranged a 'bonding session', which usually meant a trip to Southport or Blackpool for a couple of days. All of the lads enjoyed these breaks, because they were relaxing and stress-free. The management treated us like adults, and though we sunk a few beers, it wasn't done to excess. Having said that, my inability to hold my alcohol had meant I had to find ways of getting rid of my drinks as we sunk pint after pint and then moved on to the shorts. I began to sit only where there was a big rubber plant or something similar, so that by the time I'd had my fill, I could ditch my drink in the plant behind me. I would have been ill for days if I hadn't, because it just didn't agree with me, but I was probably the exception to the rule.

Tony Coleman – or TC, as we all called him – hadn't actually played for the club when we travelled to the Lancashire coast on this particular occasion, but he came along to get to know everyone a bit better. The hotel we were staying in had a furniture exhibition going on and after a night out we began drifting back to our beds slightly the worse for drink. TC came back and slumped on one of the exhibit couches with a cigarette in his hand. He fell asleep and the fag fell out of his hand and burned a big hole in the new suite. The manageress went ballistic when she found TC asleep on this expensive sofa and collared Malcolm the next day, demanding the damage be paid for. Mal got us all together the next day and explained what had happened and the damage that had been caused. Straight away, TC held his hand up and said, 'That was me, boss,' and Mal looked at him and said, 'TC, I'm going to have to take the manageress out and ply her with champagne and caviar to put this right, so make sure this never happens again!' He all but winked at his new protégé, and you couldn't help feeling that Mal wouldn't have wanted his wayward charge to be any different. He'd spotted something in Tony Coleman that no other manager would ever see, and he would get the very best out of him over the next couple of years. All in all, TC had made quite an impression on his first outing with the lads!

Malcolm hadn't changed a bit from my days with him at Bath and Plymouth. He was still the same larger-than-life character that I'd always known, and his coaching methods and the new ideas he was constantly introducing ranged from the odd and unusual to the inspirational and revolutionary. One thing was for sure, a coaching session with Malcolm Allison was anything but dull. One of his ideas was to bring in a specialist fitness coach – only, in typical fashion, he decided three would be better than one. He brought in Joe Lancaster, who was a long-distance runner, Derek Ibbotson, who was a middle-distance runner, and Danny Hermann, who specialised in sprint running. Mal took us to Wythenshawe Park, where they had a decent running track, and we all got stuck into our new and, as we first saw it, peculiar training routine. We'd set off on a long run around the park with Joe Lancaster, then come back to the running track, where Derek would take us for 440- and 880-metre runs, and then we'd do some sprint training with Danny. We wondered what it was all about, but gradually it took off and we found ourselves competing against each other. Because it was different, it was interesting, and making running into something most of the lads looked forward to was quite an achievement in itself. On the longer runs, Colin Bell would invariably cruise in front and Dave Connor wouldn't be far behind – I swear both of them could have run all day if they'd put their minds to it.

Then there were people like myself, who struggled on the long runs but did better on the middle-distance and sprint runs. There were three six-week sessions spread over the course of the season – always on a Monday morning – and we ended up really looking forward to them, despite our initial reservations. The methods were original back then and are still used by many coaches today, which just goes to show how far ahead of the game Malcolm was. It was all aimed at improving us as individuals and giving us an edge as a team. The running revealed a lot about each player's fitness and his individual limitations. Mike Doyle may have been as tough as old boots on the pitch but during the runs he was only OK if he was out in front. As soon as anyone overtook him, he dropped towards the back – he didn't seem to have the competitive edge to battle back and challenge at the front, which some people might be surprised to hear. Don't get me wrong, on the field of play he was dynamite and gave his all, but running wasn't his favourite part of training.

I was even used as a guinea pig by Malcolm, one time. He must have made a contact at Salford University because he informed me I was to go there and meet him for an 'experiment' of some kind. With visions of Dr Frankenstein flashing across my mind, I drove to Salford wondering what he'd discovered now – it could have been absolutely anything. He met me as soon as I arrived and we went into the university to a room where a strange-looking contraption was placed in the corner. It turned out to be nothing more sinister than a treadmill, but I'd never seen one before, so was wary when they put wires on my chest and wrist and asked me to stand on it. Malcolm said, 'We're going to start this thing up now, so just go with it.' Easy for him to say! With that, the belt started moving under my feet and, unprepared, I shot off the back and ended up spread-eagled on the floor! I dusted myself down and gave Mal a wry look. They then wired me back up and I went on it again until I gradually got the hang of it. Malcolm was also keen on players' diets and studied foods and times that would benefit us the most. Remember, all this was back in the mid-'60s and had never been done before. As I've said before, Malcolm was in a league of his own when it came to improvising methods of coaching.

Outside of the football, meanwhile, a few business opportunities had come my way during the season. I must stress, though, that I wish they bloody hadn't! They seemed like a great idea at the time, but my business acumen was all but non-existent, as I soon discovered. My attempts at earning a living aside from football, I'm sad to say, failed miserably, and each time it convinced me I'd chosen the right career. I had an opportunity to go into the table football business and I thought, 'Why not?' The first table I was involved in was placed in the Metrovicks club in Sale.

My business partner was a bloke who ran a nightclub in town. He was involved in slot machines and football tables and he thought that, because I was doing so well at City, it would be good for me to be linked in with the tables. I did my bit, but things went a bit sour with one thing and another and, after a disagreement with my business partner, we went our separate ways. It was never going to make me a millionaire, so I wasn't unduly concerned.

Not that long after, I tried my hand at the fitted furniture business, this time going in with people who I knew wouldn't let me down. My partners were my accountant, and Danny Hermann and Joe Lancaster, the two runners who Malcolm had brought in as our trainers that season. Together, we bought two big shops next door to each other on Washway Road in Sale, about two minutes' walk from my house. We got talking about one thing and another and decided we'd supply fitted furniture and put my name on the shops. Tony Book Fitted Furniture was born and we had a grand opening with lads from City and United and things went well for a while. The problem we had was that we farmed out the fitting side of the business to subcontractors, and after a while we started getting complaints in from customers, so we decided to close the shop after about a year and I decided to stick to what I knew best. At least we kept the properties, which have since become coveted business spots. We rent them out at the moment but plan to sell them in the near future and split the profit.

The end of the 1966–67 season, then, saw us comfortably clear of the relegation zone. The season also ended on a personal high for me, as I was voted Player of the Year by the Manchester City Supporters Club, in their first-ever year of running the award. On a sadder note, Johnny Crossan left City for Middlesbrough in the summer of 1967. He was my good mate, and it was such a shame to see him go. I was grateful for the hospitality and friendship he'd shown me when I first arrived. He'd been injured in a car accident and it had begun to affect his performances but, Johnny being Johnny, he had kept it all pretty much quiet instead of telling the physio and resting while his knee recovered properly. His leaving also meant a vacancy for a new captain and, in typical style, Malcolm announced it one day in the changing room before a pre-season friendly by saying to me shortly before kick-off, 'You lead them out today.' That was it – I was the new captain of Manchester City, and the other lads seemed quite happy with the decision. From then on, the lads called me 'Skip' and it pretty much stuck from that day to this.

SIX

Seasons in the Sun

'I haven't seen a better full-back in the First Division than Tony Book.'

George Best, 1969

Three-quarters of the way through our second season in Division One, and my first season as team captain, we had our first sniff of the Division One championship. On 27 March 1968, we beat one of the top contenders, Manchester United, 3–1 at Old Trafford. It had been a tremendous win against a very good side, and we walked off the pitch thinking that, if we could go to places like that and win comfortably, we really had a great chance to win the League.

We'd had a good solid season, and the introduction of Franny Lee from Bolton had given the side an extra edge, as he was such a handful in and around the box. He could hit the ball as powerfully as anyone I'd ever seen, and was a tough little so-and-so. I'd played against him for Bath City in the FA Cup, and Malcolm had asked my opinion about him prior to acquiring him. The next thing I knew, he was at Maine Road signing forms. Don't get me wrong, I think Mal would have signed Francis come what may, but it was nice to be asked, all the same. Lee was a confidence player who had a lot of belief in his own ability and was a great asset to the side over the next seven seasons.

Before Franny's arrival, it was yours truly who had volunteered to take the penalties, and the opening game of the new season had allowed me the chance to score my first goal for the club. It was 0–0 against Liverpool, in front of a crowd of almost 50,000 at Maine Road, when the referee pointed to the spot for some infringement or other. I placed the ball on the spot, walked back, jogged up and dragged it wide! The crowd booed me for my crime and I heard one bloke shout, 'Get back to Plymouth, you old bugger!' – in jest, I hoped! The game ended 0–0, so it hadn't exactly been the perfect start to the new campaign.

The United win had come several months later, but earlier in the season we had turned on the style in a number of games; none more so than for the December visit of Tottenham, later dubbed 'The Ballet on Ice'. I remember that snow had been falling heavily prior to the match, and it was a surprise it was even given the go-ahead by the referee – but once it was, we prepared as normal. The thing I most remember from that day was that, before the game, I suggested a method I'd learned from an old coach at Bath regarding footwear in the snow. I passed it on to the lads and it would give us a tremendous advantage over Spurs on the day. The Bath coach had told me to take the top layer off the leather studs to expose three small tacks underneath. I told the lads to do the same, leaving them just enough grip to be able to get a footing on the snow and ice. That was our footwear on the day and the conditions proved no problem at all for our players, throughout the ninety minutes. Regardless of the weather, in addition, we played magnificently that afternoon. Despite going behind early on to a Jimmy Greaves goal, we went on to win 4–1 with a graceful and masterful display. With the TV cameras present, it sent a message out to the watching millions that this City team was definitely going places. The Everton legend Dixie Dean had been in the press box for that game and he later told Joe Mercer, 'That's a very good team you've got there, Joe. A very, very good team.'

One of the unsung heroes of that era, and for many years into the future, was Stan Gibson, the head groundsman at Maine Road. He used to provide the perfect pitch for the team to play on, week in, week out, and he would also play his part in many home victories. Malcolm liked the grass to have a bit of zip, so he asked Stan to put water over the surface prior to a match. This made the ball travel quicker, but, of course, it also made the pitch slower and harder to run on. I'd bend Stan's ear about this, saying, 'Please keep the water off my two flanks,' and he'd laugh at me. I hated the heavy going, and liked the pitch to be just normal, without any extra water, because I was getting on a bit and the heavy pitches really took it out of me. Stan hated anyone going out on that pitch other than on match day, and you really had to suck up to him to get out there, especially if you went in his goalmouths, because he loved getting praised for the state of the playing surface. He took a lot of pride in the Maine Road pitch and I believe he was a vital part of our success.

There was another time in that 1967–68 season when we were irrepressible, and this was during our emphatic 7–0 win at Reading in an FA Cup third-round replay. I've since been told that the announcer at Elm Park said to the crowd, 'You've just seen the best team in England' as we trooped off, but I honestly can't remember it. Knowing that I was part of the best team in England was reward enough for me, and I didn't need anyone to tell me to realise it. We ploughed into the second half of the season winning many of our matches and defending solidly. We attacked with flair and had the perfect combination of skill, invention and heart throughout the team. With three games to go, we knew that if we could win them all, we'd be there. The first of the three was at home to Everton. It was a tight, tense game, with such a lot at stake for us. With the score at 0–0, I found myself on the edge of their box – nosebleed territory for me – and I let fly with a left-footed shot and watched it rocket into the top left-hand corner. It gave us a 1–0 lead, and was my first League goal for the club (I had successfully dispatched a penalty against Leicester in the FA Cup a couple of months before). We went on to win 2–0, with TC getting the killer second.

Next up were Tottenham at White Hart Lane, and that was a game we were really fired up for. We now knew that if we could win our final two matches, we would be crowned champions. It was a happy hunting ground for us and we expected to win the game. By half-time, we were 3–0 up, having given one of our best displays of the season. Confidence was high and we were flying. All of us were playing at the very peak of our game. Even though they came back at us in the second period, we never doubted we would win, but the breakneck pace of the first period caught up with us as the match wore on and we endured some terrific pressure before finally running out as 3–1 winners. That left us a trip to Newcastle United to look forward to, with the knowledge that Manchester United were hot on our heels if we made any slip-ups. United were home to Sunderland, and many felt that the pendulum had perhaps swung in their favour, considering our tough challenge at St James' Park, where few teams ever had an easy ride. We travelled to Newcastle on the Friday night before the match full of confidence, knowing that a win would guarantee the title. The whole of Manchester had been talking about the possible scenarios all week and we were just happy for the day to be finally here. We hadn't done anything differently in training, keeping to our usual routine, and that, of course, made complete sense. Joe Mercer had a saying, 'If in doubt, do nowt!'

Our hotel was in Gateshead and there was a happy, relaxed atmosphere amongst the squad. Buzzer was up to his usual tricks and Franny was bright and bubbly and telling anyone who would listen to give him the ball and he'd ensure we'd get the result. We were a group of lads who'd never won anything before and we had the hunger to be successful – we all instinctively knew this was our time and we had to make the most of it. I had no doubt in my mind that when we went out onto the pitch the next day we would be as ready and up for the challenge as we could ever be. On the day of the match, we warmed up in the dressing room until, finally, it was time to go to work and bring that championship trophy back to Maine Road. Malcolm came in and geed us all up, and Joe came in and said, 'All the best, lads.' Of course, we all rallied each other, too, because that was what we were all about. My good-luck custom was to leave my shirt off until the last possible second, and the others had their own way of preparing, too. Some would leave their shorts off, and so on. We'd have the banter for a while, but 15 minutes from kick-off we'd be serious and business-like, urging each other on.

We walked down the tunnel and onto the St James' Park pitch to a deafening roar. We couldn't believe the noise or the numbers of City fans that had made the journey – there must have been about 20,000, and our fans drowned the normally vociferous Geordies out. It was an amazing sight, and we looked around at each other and knew this was our time. We all complemented each other terrifically well and we knew our job and our role in the side. The actual game has been well documented over the years, and there's little I can say that others haven't said before but, for the record, I'll add my own brief recollection. Things gradually went our way in the match but Newcastle were always in it. Each time we edged ahead, they struck back in no time at all. It was 2–2 at half-time, but we never wavered in our self-belief and came out determined to finish the job off. We tore into the Magpies and surged in front 4–2, but they wouldn't give up, pulling a goal back to set up a frantic final few minutes. Finally, the referee blew time and we'd won 4–3 and were confirmed as champions. It was a fantastic match to take part in and our supporters poured onto the pitch from everywhere. It was difficult to absorb – here was a team that had only been promoted the season before and here we were, undeniably the best team in England barely two years later.

I was picked up by fans and carried shoulder high, allowing me to see the mass of City supporters that now covered the pitch. The Newcastle fans seemed appreciative of our achievements and stayed to applaud us, and I'm glad to say there seemed no animosity towards the team or our following. Back in the dressing room, we were told that United had lost to Sunderland, but none of it mattered – we'd done what we came to do, and that was to win the title in style, not by default. Perhaps only Manchester City could clinch the most prized trophy in the game in such a dramatic manner. Mal didn't say anything to me afterwards, but just looked at me as if to say, 'You old bugger; you've finally cracked it,' and, truth be told, I owed him everything for giving me the chance. Coming home, the City fans followed the coach all the way down the A1 to Manchester, and they trailed back as far as you could see, beeping their horns and waving scarves and rattles. It was the most memorable thing about the day for me. The bubbly was flowing all the way and Joe and Malcolm enjoyed themselves as much as we did. They had a look of paternal pride on their faces, and why not? They deserved the glory as much as any of the players.

We drove back to Maine Road and went up to the boardroom to continue the party. The drink was flowing, and an old lady who used to live next door to Stan Gibson by the ground – Mrs Dabelle – was in charge of everything upstairs and all the kitchens. It was getting late, and there was no sign of the party ending, but Mrs Dabelle had seen enough and wanted us all out. She came in, telling us as much, and Malcolm shuffled her towards a table and then, playfully, forced her under it! We were in fits of laughter because Mal wouldn't let her out for a couple of minutes. We eventually moved next door to the social club at about ten o'clock and drank into the early hours.

We paraded the trophy in a friendly against Bury a few days later at a packed Maine Road. A week after that, we were on our way to America, for what we all believed was going to be a sunshine break with a few friendly matches thrown in along the way. All the players were looking forward to the trip and, with the championship under our belts, we couldn't have been happier. It was a wind-down, as far as we were concerned, but what happened over there soon took the shine off what we had achieved. The games were tough and after a long, hard season, they were the last things we needed.

Our first two games against Dunfermline, who were on tour with us, ended in draws. The first match was held in Toronto, and it was a special night for both Malcolm and myself because the people of Toronto hadn't forgotten our time there and gave us a wonderful reception. More than 10,000 turned out, and the local press said the Toronto old boys were the main attraction of the evening! Then it was off to play Rochester, where we won 4–0. A 3–2 defeat followed against Atlanta Chiefs, who were managed by Phil Woosnam – whose father, Max, used to play for the Blues before the War – and then we lost 2–1 to German outfit Borussia Dortmund before we faced Dunfermline again in successive games. The Scottish Cup winners certainly had no intention of getting beaten by the English champions and they battled hard again to hold us to two 0–0 draws. The misery continued Stateside with another couple of defeats, when we were well beaten by Oakland Clippers and suffered a 2–1 to loss to Atlanta – the second time they'd done us on this tour. From our point of view, we were gaining nothing, and our confidence was taking a bit of a pasting. Our envisaged holiday had turned into a bit of a nightmare and we were all by this time eager to get on the plane back home.

Off the pitch, there were a few things that raised a smile or two, but I nearly lost my life as one piece of devastating news was broken to the American public. There were four of us out having drinks in some bar somewhere and we hired a cab to take us back to our hotel. On the way back, a newsflash announced that John F. Kennedy's younger brother, Bobby, had been assassinated. The woman driver seemed to go into shock and went straight through a red light, and we came within inches of colliding with another car. But for the alertness of the other driver crossing the junction at the same time, we might have been flying home in a wooden box!

A little shaken, we made it back to the hotel to discover that Joe Mercer had watched the incident on television and then phoned the chairman, Albert Alexander, in his room. Joe had said, 'I've got some sad news, Mr Alexander. Bobby Kennedy has been assassinated.' The chairman replied, 'Bobby Kennedy? What was he doing out at this time of night?' Joe had to explain that it wasn't the Bobby Kennedy that played for City but the dead President's brother!

Everyone was in tears of laughter when Joe told us. It wasn't that we were disrespectful towards what was an American tragedy – it had upset all the players, perhaps even more so because we were in the States when it happened – but the chairman's innocence and the absurdity of his response was genuinely very funny. Later on in the trip, Glyn Pardoe and I almost got left behind when we were completely forgotten about one morning. Our wake-up call never came, and I woke to discover that we had very little time to make our flight. We packed in a hurry and went down to the foyer to be told the rest of the party had left, so we scrambled into a taxi and arrived at the airport with moments to spare. I soon caught sight of Johnny Hart, who was part of the coaching staff at the time and was responsible for making sure everybody was woken up, and I gave him a right mouthful. He said he must have forgotten to knock on our room, but what was more disturbing was that nobody had even missed us! Maybe I was too quiet after all . . .

We finally headed home, tired and mentally flat from our tour. There had been too many games without a proper break in-between and, in hindsight, it was madness to make a long-haul trip after what we had achieved. We should have been allowed to put our feet up with our families and return to Platt Lane with our batteries fully recharged, ready to defend our title. I can only think that the club was offered a nice chunk of money for the tour, as was usually the case, because there was no other benefit. The crowds had been small, and the games physically demanding. I believe the actual effect it had on the defence of our title was substantial and

Joe Mercer's comment, 'Never again,' on our return said all that needed to be said.

We returned for pre-season training in July. It had been a fairly hot, dry summer and the hard ground was uncomfortable. I soon picked up what I hoped was no more than just a niggling injury, but it turned out to be much worse. My Achilles had gone and I was facing months out. It's an injury that can finish your career, but I'd suffered a couple of bad ones in the past and always battled back. The pain just came on and got worse the more I trained, and I knew it was serious, especially for a 35 year old. No doubt, many thought it might all be over for me but, having come this far, I wasn't about to let an injury stop me playing football, and I began the slow, painful journey back to fitness as the lads kicked-off the new season.

Being sidelined also meant that I would miss out on my dream of playing in the European Cup, and I count that as one of my biggest disappointments from my playing days. Joe and Malcolm included me in the party to travel to Turkey to play Fenerbahce, who were our opponents in the qualifying round. We were expected to beat them comfortably over the two legs, but the Turks had proved to be a tough test at Maine Road, holding us to a 0–0 draw, despite us being all over them and having a host of good chances. Malcolm's pre-match statement that we would 'terrify Europe' looked likely to come back and haunt him unless the lads could turn things around in the second leg. It was scorching hot when we arrived in Turkey, and after a night's rest at the hotel we were staying in I opened the curtains and could see the stadium we'd be playing at, which was down in the valley. It was about 8.30 a.m. and there were already huge queues to get in!

I watched the training session and, later, travelled to the game with the lads. On the short coach trip to the ground, we passed armed police and it was a bit unnerving to think they were there to protect us as much as anything. There was a good turn-out of City fans in the ground but it was a very hostile atmosphere, all the same. Though we scored first, through Tony Coleman, the Turks built up a head of steam and stormed back to win 2–1 on the night, to dump us out at the first hurdle. It was a major shock at the time that the English champions should be out so early, especially with Manchester United's recent triumph in the competition. The way things were going in the 1968–69 League, I had to resign myself to probably never appearing in the European Cup as a player.

I was put in plaster for a month, and, although I tried to get going again, the pain was still too much. I just couldn't seem to shake it off and, as weeks went by without any improvement, Malcolm told me he was going to play me in a reserve match at Maine Road, around November. He told me he would have the club surgeon, Mr Rose, at the game as well, to see how things went. I agreed to play and strolled through the first half without getting too involved, but in the second half I made a challenge and my Achilles went on me again, probably worse than before.

Mr Rose examined my leg in the dressing room and then injected cortisone directly into my wounded Achilles. It was excruciatingly painful and, unfortunately, it didn't work. It was a worrying time for me and my family, as all efforts failed to improve on the injury and I wondered if my career might be coming to a premature end, after all. The club didn't want to operate on it, and that again made me wonder if perhaps they knew something they weren't telling me. It must have been December when it was suggested that I should have a course of radiotherapy, to see if that would help. I was a little concerned about the idea, but I had nothing to lose, so I booked in at Christies Hospital in Didsbury and had my first dose. I rested for a few days after, no doubt driving Sylvia mad because I was a pain in the backside to have around the house. I was bad-tempered and frustrated, but the radiotherapy seemed to be easing the pain.

I played in a friendly against Crook Town just before Christmas 1969 and took things gently during the game. To my relief, I got through it without any adverse effects. I was soon back into the training and in early January I was selected for the FA Cup match at Newcastle. Again, I came through it without any problems. My Achilles felt fine and things returned to normal. I was relieved to be back but disappointed by the manner in which we'd lost to Fenerbahce. I consoled myself with the thought that I was lucky to be still playing the game I loved after being out for so long.

The FA Cup provided our only – if you could call it 'only' – silverware for this season. The semi-final paired us with Everton and we travelled down to Villa Park the day before to settle in at our hotel. We had our evening meal and our coach, big Dave Ewing, came to my table and sat next to me. I think he could sense something I had always believed I didn't really suffer from – nerves – and he asked me if I fancied a stroll around the hotel grounds. We chatted as we walked and came to a nearby pub. Dave asked if I fancied a pint. I'd never taken a drink before a game but this was our coach asking me so I said it couldn't do any harm and we went in. I had my usual – a Mackeson's Stout – and we left for the hotel again. The drink relaxed me and I had a great night's sleep. It might not have been textbook advice, but it was the best remedy to my nerves and it highlighted that good coaching is not necessarily confined to the training pitch.

The match itself was a difficult one but we were always in with a shout. Dave Connor did a magnificent job of snuffing out Alan Ball, as he had done in previous clashes with Everton, and this prevented them from creating any clear-cut opportunities. The longer the game went on, the more we fancied nicking something, and the thing that sticks in my mind from this game was the late winner from our young defensive midfielder, Tommy Booth. There were only a few minutes left and you could see on the Everton lads' faces that they knew there was no way back. We celebrated in the dressing room and the chairman, Albert Alexander, came down to see us. He was made up.

'Well done, lads!' he said. 'Magic! Absolutely fantastic! You know we'll make a few quid from this and we'll be able to go out and buy some good players.' All the lads' jaws hit the floor. Talk about back-handed compliments! Mr Alexander was in his 70s and was a great character, but his tact and timing were somewhat misplaced on this occasion.

Our League form was still nothing to write home about but one trip – away to Southampton – sticks in the memory, though not for the football. We'd been well beaten 3–0 by the Saints at The Dell and we returned to our hotel to try to unwind and forget the performance by having a few drinks in the bar. One of the younger squad members copped off with this girl at our hotel and took her back to his room – I'll leave the rest to your imagination. What he didn't realise, I found out later, was that his room was next to Joe Mercer's! A rather bleary-eyed Joe wandered down for breakfast and said to Malcolm, 'I don't know what they were bloody doing in the room next to me but there was banging on the wall all night and their blasted headboard wouldn't stop creaking, either.' It would have had to be Joe in the next room!

So we'd made it to the FA Cup final, where we would face a Leicester City side that were struggling against relegation in the League. The build-up to the final was so relaxed it is hard to describe. We travelled down on the Wednesday before, and on the Thursday evening we all went to the Football Writers' Dinner.

I didn't think Joe and Malcolm would let more than a few of us go but we went *en masse* to this prestigious event, which showed how laid-back they were about the final. It was fantastic for me, personally, because my teammates were all there to support me on what was a fantastic evening. I had received a letter not long before, informing me that I'd been voted joint Football Writers' Association (FWA) Footballer of the Year with Dave Mackay. I must admit, I had reckoned that my best chance of winning the award had come in the previous season, when I'd done well and captained the team to the League championship. This season, I'd missed half through injury and we'd finished halfway down the League. In our League-winning year, however, United had won the

European Cup, and the award had gone to George Best, so I certainly didn't have any argument with that. The only way I can work it out is that they put our 1967–68 League triumph together with the fact that we'd reached the FA Cup final in 1969. Also, they perhaps thought I deserved something for coming back from a long absence through injury to help the lads get to the final. It was the first time the award had ever been shared, and it remains the only time it's happened to this day. Dave said at the time, 'That's great. Two old men together,' and I knew where he was coming from. There's many a good tune played on an old violin, as the saying goes! I was told later that two votes had arrived too late to be included and, had they been counted, they would have made one of us a clear winner.

I had a lot of respect for Dave Mackay, as he was a tremendous player with a lot of good qualities. I was very proud of the award but I didn't look for individual accolades – I would have preferred it to have been awarded to all the lads. It would have sat more comfortably with me because it was a team game and that's how I saw it. In all honesty, I'm not the best speaker in the world and have never sought the limelight, because I'm basically quite shy. My strength was out on the pitch, in the thick of things, and my best asset was the ability to read situations before they happened. As I said, we stayed out late and had a great night and, though I'm not sure it's the done thing before such an important match, Joe and Malcolm clearly wanted me to enjoy this moment and there was no stuffiness or treating us all like kids. We played hard and worked hard, and that was all that counted.

Along these same lines, the management took us out to a Chinese restaurant on the Friday evening, literally hours before the big day kick-off. We could eat whatever we wanted – there were no restrictions – and by the Saturday we were in a wonderful frame of mind.

We were waiting in the dressing rooms to be given the OK to prepare to go out but, when it came, we decided to hang back a minute and let Leicester stew for a few moments. The fans were amazing that day and I wasn't quite prepared for all the colour and noise of the huge, ecstatic crowd when we walked out through that tunnel. The experience made the hairs on the back of my neck stand up.

The match itself was close enough, but we never thought of defeat, so when Buzzer made his way to the by-line, then dragged the ball back to Neil Young, Youngy cracked a shot past the Leicester goalkeeper and into the roof of the net from around 10 yards out. Both teams had their chances, but Young's goal was worthy of winning any final. To appear in an FA final, let alone to actually win it, was a dream come true. It wasn't that long since I'd been earning my wage with Bath City and here I was, 35 years of age, lifting the most famous cup in the world. For me, it was like being Roy of the Rovers and I just let it all sink in as we paraded the Cup around Wembley. Moments like these make all the blood, sweat and tears during your career worthwhile, and they don't come along in your life too often.

I recall that Malcolm Allison was banned from the bench on this fantastic day, so he was sitting up in the stand, behind the bench, throughout the match. I was told later that every time the Leicester City winger, Len Glover, got the ball and attacked me, Malcolm stood up, shouting, 'Two-to-one Bookie! Two-to-one Bookie!' That's how he was – if he believed in you he'd let the world know . . . one way or another.

My entire family, save for Rodney, who was away with the Army, had travelled down from Bath that day and it was one of the proudest days of my life. Knowing they were there and being able to share the experience with them was incredible and unbelievably fulfilling.

One of the things I noticed is how it all passed by so quickly. One minute you're kicking off, the next you're holding the Cup, then you're getting changed and off to a reception and then it's on to the train for the journey home. It's only later on that you have time to reflect and replay the events in your mind. We arrived at Wilmslow and got on the open-top bus for a drive to the Town Hall. The fans were everywhere. The streets were packed from Wilmslow to St Anne's Square and the reception in Albert Square was unbelievable. Thousands upon thousands must have turned out to see us home and none of us will ever forget it. Joe and Malcolm said a few words to get the crowd going and I just thanked everyone for their fantastic support.

That was the end of the season for us and I went home to relax by having a quiet family summer with Sylvia and the kids. I felt like I still had a few years left in me and was determined to come back as fit and strong as I'd ever been. I suppose around this time, if I'm honest, I was hoping for a late call into the England side. As a club, we'd been going fantastically well, and I was playing the best football of my career, but I was disappointed not to have at least got a look-in on just one occasion. Sir Alf Ramsey never made contact with me, but I suppose my age was the main reason for that. I was around 35 and maybe it was difficult for Sir Alf to see me as a player he could use for more than the odd game before I passed my sell-by date. It just wasn't to be, but I would have been the proudest man alive to be called upon to represent my country. There is, at least for me, a nice postscript to this, and it came from former City captain Sam Barkas, who used to come and watch us play whenever he could, and then seemed to take an even bigger interest when I took over as manager. Sam would often stop by my office for a quick chat, and one day he came in and said, 'Tony, I always thought you should have got an England cap, so I'd like you to accept this.' He then passed me one of the England caps he'd won as a player. I thought it was a lovely gesture and I've still got the cap tucked away safely.

Another wonderful tribute came from Joe Mercer. There was a lot of talk about the England squad for the 1970 World Cup in Mexico, and whether I was too old to be considered. Joe thought not and made an impassioned plea for me to be included. He said that he would gladly get knocked out of the two cup competitions in which City were progressing well, in exchange for me earning a cap for my country, which I thought was an incredible thing for any manager to say about one individual.

'I have a great deal of respect for Sir Alf Ramsey,' said Joe, 'so I wouldn't presume for one moment to attempt to teach him his job. But I still think Tony Book is the best full-back in Britain.

'If a man is the best player in England at the time, irrespective of age, there should be no discrimination. He has all the qualities a defender needs to make a success of his job. He senses danger and inspires everybody around him.'

What better praise could a player get than to have such a testimonial from a man like Joe? It didn't change Sir Alf's mind, but nobody can take those words away from me.

SEVEN

A Team for All Seasons

> 'What a great game he had today. He's 32, you see,
> and people think you're finished then. He certainly
> showed them today.'
>
> Joe Mercer, 1966

Just as had happened at the beginning of our title defence season, the 1969–70 campaign began inconsistently again, with mixed League-form. The first player of this season's side to leave was on his way after a brief – but certainly not dull – stay at Maine Road. Tony Coleman left for Sheffield Wednesday in October and, as far as I understand, there was nothing acrimonious in the move – he was just a drifter and he needed a new challenge. He'd left an indelible image on us all with his wit and talent, and the place was a little quieter without him – a lot quieter, in fact.

We started the campaign like a house on fire, thrashing Sheffield Wednesday 4–1 at home, but we then lost the next three – two of them to Liverpool, who were just beginning to take off under Bill Shankly. Young Ian Bowyer was coming on in leaps and bounds and scored five goals in the first seven League games, but later in his career he would come in for some rough treatment from the

City fans, and it was something that really disappointed me. I can only think it was because some of the crowd didn't feel he was a Manchester City-type player. He eventually left for Nottingham Forest, where he was a huge success and the driving force behind two of their European Cup successes. He was a good kid, who'd come through the ranks, and perhaps he'd broken into our team when we were just starting to tail off a bit. Despite winning three and drawing three of the next six, we were still off the leading pack and it took a terrific run of six wins out of the next ten to put us back in with a shout again. Christmas and New Year did little for our title hopes, though, with an awful spell of five defeats out of six and the League was now looking out of our grasp. We'd dropped too many points already and, though in today's system we could have possibly kept on the leaders' trail, it was only two points for a win back then and the gaps were much harder to close. At least we had qualified for the European Cup-Winners' Cup (ECWC), and I finally had the chance to play against some of the top continental clubs. We progressed well through the early rounds of this tournament. Thanks to our FA Cup triumph, we were now preparing to take on Spanish side Atletico Bilbao, who were, ironically, managed by an Englishman, Ronnie Allen. We flew out to play them and were soon wondering whether we were cut out for European competition as we quickly went 2–0 down. We couldn't let them get any further away from us or we'd never be able to turn the tie around, so we dug in deep and eventually settled down and started to play our natural attacking game.

It was one of the hardest matches I'd ever played in, as the Spaniards ripped us apart in the first half. They were outstanding, but we came back in the second half and pulled a vital goal back. They came back at us again and went 3–1 up, but by the final whistle we had pulled level at 3–3 – a wonderful result for us, and a moral victory, psychologically. If they could play so well and still only end up drawing, they must have realised we were a bit tasty, too. I remember Tommy Booth had been ill with a stomach upset when we flew out and was still unwell on the day of the game, but he played magnificently and scored a goal, too – Tommy Steel, I always thought of him as.

I'd enjoyed my first European scrap and I'd learnt a lot from that game. I knew that if you could get really at them on their own turf, you would always be in with a chance. Basically, in Europe, you have to do anything you can not to lose the away leg. The return game was completely different. We blew them away 3–0 to earn the right to play Belgian side SK Lierse in the next round. We breezed past them 8–0 on aggregate and went on to the next round, where an unknown Portuguese outfit stood between us and a place in the semi-finals. Quietly, we were also making good progress in the League Cup and had seen off the Merseyside trio of Southport, Everton and Liverpool (who we'd played three times in six weeks). If anything, we were becoming a cup side, possibly because of the make-up of the team. We wanted to go out and entertain and play the game the way it should be played and it just so happened that this mentality was better suited to the knockout situations when we automatically slid up a gear. In fact, I don't think we could play any other way. Joe and Malcolm wanted us to play total football. They wanted us to attack and excite fans, so our game was all about going forward and trying to score goals.

We saw off QPR 3–0 at Maine Road and moved into the 1969–70 League Cup semi-finals, where we faced Manchester United over two legs. Doyley was stirring things up as usual and I was up against George Best again, but we won the first game 2–1. United knew they had a great chance of finishing the tie off at Old Trafford and we were trailing 2–1 in the second game when we were awarded an indirect free kick on the edge of the box. Franny had a crack and Alex Stepney instinctively saved the shot. Buzzer's instincts, however, were razor sharp too, and he nipped in to poke the rebound home for 2–2. We were on our way to Wembley for the second successive season, and it was all the sweeter to have beaten our rivals and left them dreaming of what might have been.

Back in Europe, we'd pulled Academica Coimbra out of the hat. As I said, they were a bit of an unknown quantity and I remember flying out to Portugal and stepping off the plane at Faro Airport to find the weather warm, with beautiful blue skies. Not exactly what we'd left behind at home, where we were having a freezing spring. It was a treat to be there and train in the sunshine, and it reminded me of my time in Canada, which brought back a lot of happy memories. Academica, however, proved to be no evening stroll in the sun. They were a really tough outfit – a university team made up of young players – and we just about managed to grind out an energy-sapping no-score draw, giving us a great chance in the second leg. We left the warmth of the Portuguese spring to return to the wintry conditions at home, with much of the country under a blanket of snow. Our flight was diverted from London, where we were meant to be preparing for the League Cup final against West Bromwich Albion, to Birmingham. We had to get a coach to London and we didn't arrive until the early hours of Thursday morning. I was carrying a dead leg at the time, and Joe Mercer, being an Arsenal legend, was able to send me to Highbury for treatment on it, which my leg responded to fairly well.

I was desperate not to miss the final but was shocked to see the state of the Wembley pitch, which was in an appalling condition. The Horse of the Year Show had been held earlier that week and the pitch was no more than a mud bath underneath its covering of snow. Joe called it 'a pig of a pitch', and he was right. As I stated earlier, I hated the heavy going, so these conditions couldn't have been worse as far as my old legs were concerned. Whether it would sap more energy out of our already tired squad remained to be seen. We were instructed to play our normal game and to go out and entertain.

We went behind to a Jeff Astle goal on six minutes and went in still 1–0 down at the break. We went into the dressing room and I remember Franny saying, 'Do we want to win this game or not? Because, if we do, you want to start getting the ball in to my feet.

I'll win it for you.' That was the confidence we had in the team at the time, and that's why we were so good in cup competitions, because we could focus on the job in hand. We went out recharged, and it was actually Doyley who pulled us level, and then his good mate, Glyn Pardoe, won it in extra time. It was an incredible time for the club, fans and players and we'd added another trophy to our rapidly filling cabinet.

Our defence of the FA Cup lasted only until our second draw, when Manchester United gained vengeance for the League Cup by beating us comprehensively, 3–0, at Old Trafford. There were still a fair number of League games to go, and a European trophy to have a crack at, and we were determined to finish on a high. Coimbra arrived at Maine Road and, to their credit, gave us another tough examination, but a Tony Towers goal won it for us in added time to set us up with German side Schalke 04 in the semi-final. We kept the first leg tight and came back with a creditable 1–0 defeat, giving us a great chance of finishing the job off at Maine Road. We then achieved this in magnificent style, beating them 5–1, which got us into the final. It was yet another fantastic occasion to look forward to and I couldn't wait to be the first captain to lead Manchester City out in a major European cup final. Now we'd got this far, we didn't even consider defeat as a possibility. We knew the Gornik Zabrze team we'd be facing would be tough – no mugs made it to the final – but we fancied ourselves against anyone. On our day, I reckoned we could turn anybody over, and I mean anybody.

The League was still vitally important, but it was hard for some of the lads to get motivated for what were now fairly meaningless games. Two wins out of ten proved that we'd taken our eye off the bread and butter games and were, perhaps subconsciously, saving our best for the cups. But there was still a spark of controversy to come, towards the end of the season. We were at a hotel when one of the lads received two phone calls within a short period of time. One was from a manager of another club offering the lads money to lose a match. Incredibly, the second call was from somebody else offering us money to win the game! In each case, the requested result would have benefited their clubs in various ways, but I can't name either the clubs or the people who contacted us, for obvious reasons. Our player came and told us what had been said, but nobody was interested and we never would have been. For one, it was not the way we went about things and, for another, we would never cheat our supporters or our fellow professionals. Had the FA got wind of what was going on at that time, the two callers and clubs they represented would have had the book thrown at them and would probably have been relegated a couple of Divisions. Back then, with the wages fairly meagre, some players may possibly have considered it. It just didn't apply to our lads and, so far as I know, that was the only occasion anything underhand like that ever happened. For the record, I believe we won the match in question.

With the League programme wrapped up and a final placing of tenth in the table, we arrived in Austria and settled into our Vienna hotel. The training went well and the weather was pleasant on the day of the game, with blue skies all the way up to kick-off. Then the heavens opened and torrential rain poured for the rest of the night! There was no cover for the 9,000 City fans in the Prater Stadium who had made the journey, and likewise for our wives and the club officials. In truth, the venue was not the best for a major final but it didn't get our supporters down. Let's face it, hardy Mancunians are not going to let a bit of rain – all right, a lot of rain – bother them too much are they?

On the other hand, we loved the conditions because they suited our style down to the ground. Gornik were useful, make no mistake about it, and, in their international forward Lubianski, they had a world-class performer. We just had too much for them on the night, however. We had players like Franny Lee, Neil Young and Mike Summerbee who loved the big occasion and had the talent to make the most of these games. Buzzer was injured that night and was replaced by Ian Bowyer. We lost Mike Doyle early on with an ankle injury, too, but we still went on to win 2–1 – and I got to lift another piece of silver. We had a real knees-up in Vienna afterwards, and I recall we had a sing-song with the chief scout, Harry Godwin, who was a fair talent on the piano, at the end of the night.

We returned home to a heroes' welcome, drunk on success, and paraded the trophy in front of thousands of City fans in Albert Square. United may have won the European Cup a couple of years earlier, but we had become the first English team to win a domestic trophy and a European cup in the same season. We'd got to the stage where we knew we were going to win any final we reached because we were that good. Malcolm claimed we were going to go and play on the moon, because we could beat anyone, anywhere, anytime. We were probably one of the best cup teams ever, and, although our League form was patchy, the only time we'd been consistent in the League we'd won that too. The European success was another page in what had become a fairy tale for me and I used to wonder sometimes why it was all happening the way it was. It also crossed my mind more than once that if I had broken into League football when I was younger, I may have missed all these wonderful years with City.

It wasn't long before we headed off for an end-of-season tour to Australia, which was the best tour of my life. We treated it as a holiday and, though we played well enough, there was this old reporter who'd emigrated from England years back who gave us a load of stick throughout the tour. Everywhere we went, the hotels we stayed at always had three bottles of pink champagne in our bedroom fridge so we just relaxed and went with the flow. The sponsors of the tour, some tobacco company, really looked after us and, with two trophies in the bag, what were we expected to do? We were out there a month in what was supposed to be their winter. So much for that, we were sitting around the pool every day in our trunks sipping beers and eating from the barbie. Buzzer was in plaster because he had a broken leg and we had to carry him around everywhere. Despite that, he did a load of club PR work by attending several supporters club meetings. Where he went on his travels in-between, God only knows, but he wasn't one for sitting in an armchair with a good book! Australia is a fantastic country and we all left with fond memories of the place.

We had a brief rest at home and then it was back to business for the 1970–71 season. In all fairness, it wasn't a memorable campaign. It would be the first time since 1967 that we didn't win anything, despite almost defending our ECWC title. The crowds were dipping slightly, due to our inconsistency in the League, and the team had definitely peaked as a unit. One game that sticks out was the ECWC tie with Linfield, from Northern Ireland. They may have been a part-time outfit but they gave us a real fright. We were expected to beat them easily but only won 1–0 at Maine Road and, as sides like that often did, they lifted their game significantly to win 2–1 at their home ground, but we scraped through on away goals. We saw off Honved before facing Gornik again. We lost the first leg 2–0 but won the second by the same score, leading to a play-off in Copenhagen (miles away from either of our grounds). They must have been sick of the sight of us and we did them again, 3–1, to go though to the semi-finals to face Chelsea, probably the last team we wanted out of the hat. We had a lot of players missing through injury: key players such as Colin Bell, Mike Doyle, Glyn Pardoe and both Tommy Booth and Mike Summerbee missed at least one of the games. We lost both legs 1–0 and were resigned to not winning anything but, considering the previous years, maybe that was to be expected. The team was ageing, and it was hard to maintain the kind of performance level we had set for ourselves. I still had enough in me for one or possibly two more years as a player and, at 36, I still felt I had a lot to offer. I was still playing catch-up and, in my mind, I was only now approaching 30. Trouble is, your body doesn't always go along with your enthusiasm. The seasons would get harder from here on in.

EIGHT

All Good Things . . .

'The older you get, the harder you have to work. Tony
realised this a long time ago and I've never known a
more dedicated athlete.'

Freddie Griffiths, City Physiotherapist, 1974

Around the start of the 1971–72 season, I became aware of a man
who would play his part in changing the hierarchy at Maine Road
and, in his own way, affect the way the club was run for many,
many years. I was parking my car on the day of a match in the
players' car park when a Rolls-Royce pulled up close by. A smartly
dressed gent got out and I made a comment to him about his motor
and he smiled and said, 'Yes, it is nice, isn't it? You'll be seeing a lot
more of both the car and me from now on.' He then strolled
through the main entrance in his fur coat and bowler hat. The man
was Joe Smith, who had joined the board and obviously had some
big ideas. It was the first inkling I had that there were imminent
changes 'upstairs'. I later became friendly with Joe and his wife,
Connie. Our two daughters went to the same school and Joe and
his wife took the girls away on summer holidays together. Joe, who,
I'm told, introduced double-glazing to these shores, was being lined

up to become the next chairman of City, but ill-health eventually forced him to quit the board and take things easier. His arrival had, however, begun a chain of events that would eventually lead to Peter Swales becoming the chairman.

As time went on, internal club politics began to surface every now and then, and at the Annual General Meeting of that year the board of directors asked if I'd go along and speak on their behalf and back them up if there were any demands from those gathered to change things on the board. The directors wanted to keep things the way they were and they must have thought having me on board would calm any disenchantment. So a director signed over one single share to me to make things all official and I went along, signed my name and sat in the room with all the shareholders. I wasn't into the politics of the club and it was all a bit strange. I sat there and listened to the manager and the Q & A session and that was about it. I didn't get involved because these people had a right to express their views and I wasn't about to play the role of defender of the board. As it turned out, it was hardly riveting stuff, but I was there in a sort of official capacity and, if nothing else, I'd earned the right to be called a club shareholder . . . so I thought!

I left the social club and headed back to my car when I heard footsteps approaching from behind. It was Sydney Rose, the director who'd signed the single share over to me and, completely out of breath, he said, 'Tony, sign that share back over to me, will you?' I started to smile, because I thought he was joking, but it soon became apparent that he wasn't. I signed the piece of paper he had brought with him and officially gave him his share back – crafty bugger – and that was the beginning and end of my time as a City shareholder. Later, the directors asked me what had gone on and they obviously thought I was level-headed enough to give a balanced account of the evening but, in truth, there wasn't much to tell. After that, I decided to give the AGMs a wide berth, unless I absolutely had to go along to one in whatever official capacity I was in at that time.

I was 37 years of age going into the 1971–72 campaign but I was still in good nick. I wasn't about to let age get in the way because I was enjoying myself too much. I was holding down a position and I was doing all right, so I wasn't about to give it all up voluntarily. Joe and Malcolm would rest me every now and then, but, generally, if I was fit, I played. Everyone – including me – knew that the clock was ticking but, for me, age didn't matter. If a young kid of 17 comes in and does well, he should be in the team. It was the same with an old pro like me. You have to play the best men you have and, fortunately, the management decided I was the best option more often than not.

We'd had pretty much the same side for seven years now, with just the occasional new signing here and there. Great teams stay great by just replacing the odd player every now and then, to maintain the side's strength and not upset the general rhythm and shape that has made them successful in the first place. Liverpool did it throughout the 1970s and Manchester United did it in the 1990s. In the 1960s, City did it, and all three clubs have been phenomenally successful in the process. We signed big Wyn Davies from Newcastle in the close season and he soon settled into the side and forged a good partnership with Franny Lee. Wyn was a good player, who I first played against in my days with Bath when we played Bolton in the FA Cup. I'd faced him a number of times since then and I knew he was a real handful for defenders. He was good in the air, had a good temperament and fitted in well with the lads. We'd never had a target man before because it had always either been Franny on his own or Buzzer or Youngy up there with him. You could play long balls up to Wyn and he'd win the header most times, or lay the ball off well, and he was a constant threat at set pieces.

My relationship with Malcolm was good, but, Franny Lee aside, he never confided in me when he was about to sign players or let them go – that wasn't what our relationship was about at all. He was the coach and I was a player, and that was that, which is what I expected. I may have been the senior pro and played for Big Mal at several clubs, but that didn't entitle me to be privy to what was going on behind the scenes and that's the way I liked it. In fact, I didn't realise that Joe and Malcolm would be heading their separate ways in the not too distant future. Malcolm was always his own man and loved to build empires that he had control over. That wasn't quite the case at City because he was assistant to Joe and you had to wonder just how long he was prepared to stay as number two. He wanted people to know what he'd done for the club and clearly felt that he wasn't getting the credit he deserved. He was at the top of the tree for coaching, as far as I was concerned, but, as for managing the team, well, that's a different kettle of fish altogether.

We learned through the press that Joe was moving 'upstairs' and Malcolm was taking over full control of the team affairs and everything else. In that respect, it didn't feel that different, because he was still coaching us as normal. It was sad to see Joe having to take a back seat because I'm sure it's not what he wanted. He was a wonderful, gentle man who put City right up there with the very best, and he deserved better than the way he was treated at the end. He may have been more like a figurehead for the club and wonderful PR man, but he was absolutely vital to the partnership, make no mistake about it. I didn't feel that City did right by Joe, and neither did anyone else I knew, but we didn't have much of a say in the affair and just had to get on with it.

That season, Franny was banging goals in for fun. He had also scored a hatful from the penalty spot and was forever being accused of diving. He was a clever player, but not a cheat – he just had the ability to make the most of a situation. Having said that, he did do the odd dying swan!

One of the best games that season was the Maine Road derby with Manchester United. Sammy McIlroy was making his debut for the Reds as a young kid and they were going along quite well, as I recall. There was always something happening on or off the ball in these games and this match was no exception. Things kicked-off once or twice around the pitch that afternoon, but the game itself was a fantastic spectacle for the fans, ending 3–3.

The season was ambling along quite well and we were putting in a decent challenge at the top but I became the subject of, shall we say, 'crowd displeasure', for what seemed, to me at least, the first time. It was over before it had really begun, but it started during a home game with Leicester City in December 1971. I played a poor back pass and Foxes striker Keith Weller nipped in to score past Joe Corrigan. A section of the crowd was on my back straight away, booing my every touch thereafter, but we ended up taking a point in a 1–1 draw. Obviously, we're not talking about the whole crowd, or I would have been devastated, but there were a few voicing their opinions, all the same. I didn't let it get to me and got my head down in training and concentrated on the next game, which was just after Christmas, at Stoke City. We played well that day and I even managed to get on the score-sheet in a 3–1 win. The jeering stopped before it had really started, but it made me realise, after all the success we'd enjoyed in recent years, how fickle some individuals could be and how short their memories were. I believe the age factor must have come into it, too, when we had a bad game. People were bound to point the finger at me, being the oldest in the team, and they'd wonder whether I could still cut the mustard. That's life, I'm afraid, and it's the fans' prerogative. The bottom line was, if I hadn't made the mistake in the first place, they wouldn't have booed me at all. It was my one and only experience of the section the journalists refer to as the 'boo boys', but you sometimes have to experience things like that to understand it better, especially as I became manager, later on.

Going into March 1972, we were top of the table and felt we could go and win the title once again. All the teams were tightly packed, but we'd been consistent in the League for the first time since we'd won the championship in 1968 – no doubt because we'd exited both knockout competitions early on and could concentrate better on the job in hand. Then, Malcolm signed Rodney Marsh from QPR. There was a lot of hype in the press surrounding his imminent arrival, which dragged on for about three weeks before he finally became a City player. From a personal point of view, I'd always felt – and still do – that Rodney had all the ability in the world, but the problem he had when he arrived was that he was unfit. No doubt he'd been hoping the move would come off sooner and maybe had eased up in training at QPR. That can happen to anyone. I can sympathise with him in that respect, but he hadn't kept himself at peak fitness and he'd just joined a side whose game was based around being at optimum levels of stamina.

It was a mistake to play him straight away. Malcolm should have worked with him in training for a month and got his sharpness back and also let him get to know the lads and how they played. Then he could come in for the final push for the championship – but Malcolm wanted him in straight away, and young Tony Towers, who'd been playing out of his skin, was dropped to make way. Tony was only a young kid and he accepted it well. All the lads told him his time would come again, and it did. We beat Chelsea on Rodney's home debut but then failed to win the next three. Stoke beat us 1–0 at home and Gordon Banks was in a class of his own during that match, saving everything we threw at him.

Next up was a trip to The Dell, where we rarely picked up anything ever, and the 2–0 defeat to Southampton severely dented our hopes for the League. We rallied to beat West Ham at Maine Road, and then Manchester United at Old Trafford, and there was still just a point or two separating the top four teams – City, Leeds, Liverpool and Derby County. Our main undoing in this campaign had been our failure against these three rivals. We travelled to Coventry City having been beaten just six times in the campaign, but four of those defeats had been administered by Leeds (twice), Liverpool and Derby County. Just one win from those games would have made a tremendous difference at the end, but there was huge controversy to come in our final couple of games on the road. With three to play, we were held at lowly Coventry City 1–1 and our three rivals went above us in the table. It was another hammer blow and meant that anything but a victory at Ipswich Town would guarantee we were out of the running. We were pumped up for that match and Ipswich had nothing really to play for, except pride. We'd beaten them 4–0 at Maine Road in December, and they clearly wanted to avenge that result and were anything but pushovers. We were unlucky that day, with Wyn Davies picking up a nasty head injury, and I got into a spot of bother myself. Colin Bell had a goal chalked off and, as we walked off Portman Road, I found myself alongside the referee, who was in my path of entering the dressing room. As I passed him, I elbowed him in the chest and he kicked up a big fuss, which caused Wyn to rush out, fists raised, ready to fight the referee. The reason for the scuffles had been the disallowed goal, because Bell's strike had been a corker and definitely should have stood. With the scores level at that point, it almost certainly would have won us the game, and a chance of a victory that would have kept us in the hunt for the title, albeit as rank outsiders. We subsequently lost our concentration, however, and lost the match 2–1.

We were gutted on the journey home because Derby had won, giving them a three-point cushion with only two points left to play for. Still, in our final match of the season, we beat Derby, managed by the irrepressible and youthful Brian Clough, 2–0 at Maine Road. It proved a point to the 55,026 crowd – and to ourselves – that, if anything, we'd lost the championship rather than had it taken away from our grasp. It's hard to say whether Rodney's arrival cost us the title but, in my own opinion, we shouldn't have changed a winning side. I'm not sure what would have happened had he not signed and we'll never know for sure, but maybe it's a little unfair to place the blame squarely on his shoulders. I'm almost certain that he himself wanted a little time before being pitched in, but it just didn't happen. That was the end of another season for me and a hugely disappointing one, considering how things had looked at one point. I would be 38 years old in a few months and, realistically, I knew it would be difficult to challenge for the title again because our team was ageing and, in many ways, this was one last hurrah for a good number of us. I still felt good, but I wondered now just how long I had left in top-flight football. Derby were deservedly crowned champions by virtue of a single point over Leeds, Liverpool and ourselves, and we ended fourth in the League, with the worst goal average of the latter three.

A few weeks later, I had to face the FA and answer the referee's report in front of a panel. Wyn got away with it because they said he didn't know what he was doing owing to slight concussion – a touch of genius from the big man – but when I went in, they asked if I would like the panel to take the rest of my career into consideration. I couldn't remember too many bad points down the years, so I said, 'Please do.' I reckoned it might help my cause. Surely the seven years I'd been playing League football at Plymouth and City would show a pretty clean record? I could have sworn I saw a wry smile on the officials' faces after I'd said that, because the slippery buggers went back to my amateur days and reminded me I'd been sent off four times previously! My bright idea meant I would now have to serve a two-match suspension at the start of the next season.

It was around this time that I lost my father, who died in Bath aged 81. Charlie was an Army man who loved a social drink and my mum used to say that my father could have bought us all a house if he'd kept his hand in his pocket. Dad moved into the Territorial Army and I went to his base on one occassion. As I walked in, he announced, 'That's my lad. Drinks all round.' He'd earned a lot of money during his military career but he was a spendthrift who wasted all his earnings because he wanted to enjoy himself. Typically, he'd go out about 11 a.m. Saturday morning, go to a nice hotel and have a few drinks, then go to the fishmongers and buy a couple of fresh crabs for dinner. He was generous to a fault and would do anything for any of his lads. I'd been away for such a long time that it didn't hit me as hard as it might have done if I'd been around all the time. My mum would pass away, aged 78, not long after, and they are both buried together in a Bath cemetery. I always pay them a visit when I go back to Bath.

I had to concentrate on my football again because life goes on, whether you've suffered or not – my dad had taught me that, and would have been angry with me if I'd brooded about his passing and let it interfere with my career. Football is, as they say, a great leveller, and it also brings you back to reality when you probably most need it.

Back at Maine Road, Joe Corrigan was now our first-choice goalkeeper, and, though he had some problems with his weight and form, I have never seen a goalkeeper work harder than Big Joe to improve and make himself the number one. I don't think he'd had much experience in goal when he signed for us and I think Malcolm just signed him because of his imposing stature. He was huge, measuring about 6 ft 4 in., but it was his determination to succeed that really impressed me. I could see a bit of my own spirit in Joe, because he was going to make it, come what may. He made some mistakes, like the time Ronnie Boyce volleyed his kick-out back over his head and into the net after Joe had turned to walk back to his goal-line against West Ham, but he fought hard to win over the fans and make them forget moments like that. One thing was for certain, he never turned his back on a kick down the field after that! He was a real character, too, and he used to get annoyed with us in shooting practice during training if we put one past him. He was a brilliant shot-stopper, but if anyone tried to take the piss out of him – say by chipping it over him from outside the box – he'd get mad and chase them around the pitch! He'd whack you on the muscle of your arm, and it bloody hurt as well. Malcolm did a lot of work with him and he gradually improved, lost weight and found his confidence, and eventually he represented his country and became a legend at Maine Road. He won us many games with his bravery.

Around the close season of 1972, I had to say my goodbyes to

Joe Mercer, who had decided to go to Coventry City as general manager. Malcolm was to be given total control, and the way things were done left a sour taste in the mouth. It was quite an emotional occasion, because Joe was such a lovely bloke that you never wanted him to come to any harm. He was also back to full fitness now, which was another sad thing about the whole affair. He'd suffered from ill health in his early days at City, and even from the time I arrived at the club I can recall him being a bit shaky, but he just got better and better. No doubt, the way the team had performed during his tenure had helped him along, too. I knew we were losing someone special because you don't come across too many Joe Mercers in your lifetime, believe me.

As for Malcolm, well, you don't come across many men like him, either. He'd been pushing for total control for a while now, perhaps because he felt his contributions were not being given the credit he believed they deserved. City had one of the hottest coaches in Europe, no doubt about it, and it had come to the notice of several other top clubs, including a couple from Italy and Spain. He actually went for an interview at Juventus and spent several days there on a fact-finding mission, but he ultimately turned them down and stayed with us. It was only to be expected that other sides would covet him, when you consider what he'd achieved at Maine Road.

Mal was still as inventive as ever with his coaching methods, and when he felt something out of the ordinary could benefit the team or an individual, he wouldn't hesitate to come up with an idea. This dancer Malcolm had found, Lenny Heppel, was a fleet-footed bloke with a good sense of humour. The lads enjoyed his sessions and his ideas on posture and movement. He didn't like people slouching and had the players in stitches with his camp mannerisms and so forth.

On one occasion, Lenny and Malcolm must have had a chat about Willie Donachie, who was a lovely lad, but he didn't really communicate on the pitch. He was quiet as a mouse, but he was a very good player, who Malcolm believed could be even better. So they took Willie out onto Maine Road and sent him high up to the top of the main stand. Lenny told him to shout to him in the centre circle to test his vocal strength and, though it was comical to watch, I understood what he was trying to do. To my way of thinking, however, if you are a quiet lad, that's the way you are and no amount of alternative coaching is going to change things. I liked Lenny, though, because he was good for a laugh and many of his techniques were very clever and actually worked well. He was no mug and knew what he was talking about.

We were back in Europe for the 1972–73 season, after qualifying for the UEFA Cup, and faced Spanish side Valencia in the first round. The crowds were on the decline at Maine Road – as they were at many clubs – and just 21,698 watched the first leg, which we drew 2–2. We were definitely better playing the away leg first, as we always seemed to struggle playing at home first. We lost the return 2–1, and went out on aggregate on the away goals rule. We had some young lads breaking through at this point, such as Colin Barrett and Ronnie Healey, who were occasionally getting games partly owing to the numerous injuries we had at the time. These team changes were having a knock-on effect on our League form. We didn't have a settled side during that season, and Derek Jeffries and Tony Towers, both on the first team fringes until now, made over 30 appearances each. We'd begun the season badly, losing five of the first six games, and it was always going to be an uphill struggle to win anything. We were even dumped out of the League Cup by Bury. By the tenth League game we'd won three and lost seven, including a 4–1 defeat at Birmingham City and a 5–1 thrashing by Stoke. The old team was slowly breaking up, and for our supporters who'd witnessed the most amazing era in the club's history, it must have been tough to take.

At least the FA Cup provided a little light relief, as we beat Stoke in the third round, but the draw was cruel, giving us the worst possible tie in our bid to progress – a trip to Anfield in the next round. Malcolm had been bragging in the papers about sussing 'the myth of Liverpool' out and, surprisingly, they took the bait. Trust me, Alex Ferguson isn't in the same league as Malcolm Allison when it came to playing mind games. Our trips to Anfield were always fraught occasions because we almost never got anything other than a sound beating. Bill Shankly and his fantastic backroom staff had created a machine that only thought of winning. Having said that, we were always guaranteed a warm welcome behind the scenes, partly due to the fact that Joe Fagan was there. A stalwart of the Liverpool boot-room, Joe had also played for City between 1938 and 1951, and he still had great affection for the Blues. Liverpool, though, would never let sentimentality get in the way of professionalism. Invariably, they would take you apart on the pitch, and then the backroom staff would invite you into the boot-room afterwards and laugh at you! But don't get me wrong – it wasn't malicious, just good friendly banter you hardly ever got anywhere else. The family atmosphere was perhaps the secret of their success. Our season would have been as good as over if we'd lost this match, and Malcolm knew it. He was brave to take on the might of Shanks and his bravery was rewarded. We drew 0–0 – quite a result, considering our miserable record there in the past.

Liverpool were on the way to the League title, so it was even more impressive when we finished the job off at Maine Road 2–0, in front of almost 50,000 fans. This moved us into the last 16, where we faced Sunderland. We were expected to see off Bob Stokoe's Second Division outfit – including Dave Watson and Dennis Tueart – comfortably, but drew 2–2 at home. Our hopes of a quarter-final place diminished quickly as Sunderland took us apart at Roker Park, beating us 3–1. They turned out to be quite a force to be reckoned with at that time and, of course, they went on to win that year's FA Cup (1973), beating Leeds 1–0 in one of the most famous finals ever. We were headed for a mid-table position at best as the season wore on and, in March 1973, Joe Mercer returned to a hero's reception as we took on his Coventry City side at Maine Road. Joe was loved wherever he went and he was hugely popular at Coventry, too, but no doubt he left with a wry smile, as they beat us 3–2. Not long after, there were more reports linking Malcolm with a move away – this time it was Crystal Palace. We'd seen it all before and didn't take too much notice, but it hadn't been a smooth ride for him, moving into the manager's chair. He wasn't a finance man and he wasn't the type to have a great dialogue with the board of directors, and he would invariably argue with them if they disagreed over a football matter. 'What do you know about it?' he'd ask them bluntly.

He was off with flu for a few days when relationships between him and the board were at an all-time low, and the decision was taken to sell Ian Mellor to Norwich in his absence. He was absolutely livid and, from that moment on, I knew he would leave City as soon as he had the opportunity. Peter Swales told the press that Malcolm had, in so many words, been taught a lesson because the club needed to balance the books and he'd been told to sell repeatedly. Mr Swales also added that the relationship between manager and board would now go from strength to strength. It was, in reality, the end of the relationship, and I could understand Malcolm's thinking.

The Crystal Palace link died down for a while, but Malcolm did eventually move to this London club. I always believed that certain journalists played a big part in this move. Media contacts are more powerful than they are often given credit for, and a few whispers to a chairman, encouraged by the individual looking for a particular job and further backed by stories in the papers, could often lead to all parties involved getting what they wanted. By the time Malcolm agreed to take on the job at Selhurst Park, I was in no doubt that he'd instigated it himself through his journalist pals – it was just the way things happened. He claimed he could no longer motivate the team and he was probably right. He'd done all he could and made the right decision, because selling a player behind his back was unforgivable. I was sorry to see him go, because ever since I first met him, things had gradually got better and better for me. Our paths would, of course, cross yet again in the future, but this whole affair, in my opinion, had been badly handled by the chairman and the board of directors.

NINE

Hart in the Right Place

'It simply isn't possible to play until you are 38 or 39 in the First Division. You might be able to get away with it in the lower divisions, but I doubt it. Tony was in a position that, if you use your loaf well, you can survive a little bit longer.'

Emlyn Hughes, 1974

With Joe and Malcolm's reign consigned to the history books as far as Manchester City were concerned, it was time for one of the backroom boys to take over. Johnny Hart became the new manager, and it was a move that was welcomed by the players, who all knew him well and both liked and respected him. He'd first joined the club as far back as 1944, and played for the club in the 1950s and '60s, making 178 appearances and scoring a creditable 73 goals. He had been around in one capacity or another on the coaching staff ever since his retirement. The board felt he deserved his chance and nobody argued it wasn't right to promote from within. He was a much quieter manager than Malcolm had been, and talked to the players on a more individual level. He didn't play mind games and was certainly more in the mould of Joe Mercer.

On a personal level, I was still skipper of a side that finished up in eleventh place, and I'd clocked up 29 games in the League this season – not bad, but definitely less than a season's average since I'd been at the club. I rested in the summer as much as I could, to get the weary old legs in shape, and returned for work for the 1973–74 season feeling fine and ready to go. We weren't on long contracts back then; it was more a matter of being retained, which I had been. I was still of the mind that I was playing catch up, but knew that I couldn't go on indefinitely. Age had to take its toll sooner or later, and I was well aware this could be my last campaign.

Johnny Hart was preparing for his first full season as boss and he asked me my opinion about a player he was considering signing. He wanted to know what I thought about Denis Law, who was available on a free transfer at United. Law had been at City as a kid, when Johnny was coming to the end of his time as a player. The general feeling was that Law's experience could only benefit the team. I said I thought it would be a good move all round, bearing in mind his prolific record, and the move went through, with Ken Barnes also playing a part in the transfer. It caused quite a stir at the time, and there was much consternation amongst the United supporters about Tommy Docherty allowing their hero to join City.

Things were changing for me, too. I was on the fringe of the first team and by no means an automatic choice any more, which was only to be expected. Johnny went with a couple of younger lads, like Willie Donachie and Colin Barrett, plus Glyn Pardoe had made a brave recovery from a horrific broken leg and he pretty much wore the No. 2 jersey that season. I'd come on as substitute a couple of times and played a few games in the reserves, but no more than that. I'd made up my mind I was going to see the season through, whatever the circumstances. If I was in the reserves, I'd do my best to help the youngsters – the fact that I would be almost 40 years of age towards the end of the campaign meant that it would probably be my last year as a player, anyway. But there were yet more changes ahead, because Johnny's health, which hadn't been that good in the first place, had steadily deteriorated, to the extent that he couldn't carry on in his present role at the club. The new chairman, Peter Swales, decided to appoint me as caretaker manager whilst he began a search to find a permanent replacement for Johnny, who had been forced to resign on medical advice. I took charge for the League Cup match with Walsall, and my first decision was to pick myself! I felt I was better use out on the park where I could shout instructions and actively participate rather than stand on the sidelines shouting, which, of course, I'd never done before. We drew 0–0 at their ground and brought them back to Maine Road, where I put myself as substitute and came on in what turned out to be another goalless draw. I decided to drop myself for the second replay at Old Trafford and we beat them 4–0, thanks to a hat-trick from Franny Lee, to go into the hat for the next round. I didn't play again for City.

The promotion to caretaker boss was just a progression, as far as I was concerned. I wasn't about to get too excited about it because I had a job to do and not much time to think about it. I would give it a go and see what happened but, after much soul-searching and consideration, I decided I would be better employed on the sidelines, where I could take full stock of events on the park. I enjoyed making decisions about selection and so on, even though I knew I was only filling in for whoever got the job permanently, but this was something I wanted to do and was determined to make a good go of it. I was enjoying my new role, with Dave Ewing as my right-hand man. We edged past Carlisle in the next round, with Franny scoring the only goal of the tie, and then faced York City in round three. We travelled to Bootham Crescent, where we endured a nervy goalless draw – again – but beat them 4–1 at Maine Road, with Rodney taking the match ball home on this occasion – to move into the last eight. I was aware the chairman was actively searching for a new man, so when it was announced that Norwich

City manager Ron Saunders was to be the next manager of Manchester City, I accepted the decision without any fuss because, as I said, I'd known I was only keeping the seat warm.

Saunders arrived at Maine Road and invited me into his office for a chat. He told me he wanted me to stay and to be his assistant manager, and I accepted the role without much thought. He also suggested I hang up my boots and concentrate on the job in hand, and I went along with that, too. What I should have done was said I wanted to keep playing for as long as I could, but I didn't, and he thought I'd come to the decision not to play any more on my own because I'd left myself out of several games when I was picking the team. He was in charge now and he wanted me to finish as a player when I should have at least seen the season out. It was a decision that, in retrospect, I feel we both regretted, because I think I would have been more effective for him out on the pitch every now and then, rather than sitting alongside him on the bench.

One thing I really appreciated during this transition was the support of the City lads. They formed their own committee, headed by my old mate Mike Doyle, and approached the chairman to express their desire for me to be appointed as manager. It was the kind of backing that made you feel ten foot tall, but the chairman had already had the idea of Saunders put into his mind by the influential journalist Paul Doherty. Doherty is – I believe – the man who suggested Saunders, and such was the power of the media at the time, and Doherty in particular, that his opinion alone carried great weight, especially with the chairman, who often socialised with him. Peter Swales, though, had listened to the players' views and was aware of how they felt, and it certainly made an impression on him, as I would discover a few months later.

I decided to get my head down and make my way into management by doing the best I could to assist Ron and learn as much as I could from him. I got a few extra quid for the added responsibility, but it was nothing too dramatic. Ron came in and soon stamped his personality on the place. He was a sergeant-major type – very keen on strict discipline – and he made the lads work hard in training. He was rigid in his ways, and some of the players found him hard work as a man. They had been used to being pushed to the limit in the past, but whereas there was always a light-hearted side to training with Malcolm, with Ron it was just hard work and sweat, and it wasn't going down too well. There were a lot of top established stars at City at the time and not all of them appreciated Ron Saunders' ways. There have been suggestions that, because he had come from Norwich City, he wasn't used to dealing with the calibre of players City had, but I wouldn't agree that this was the case at all. Personally, I liked the way he worked, and thought his training methods were good in the sense that he did a lot of running sessions that were beneficial to the team. He didn't do that much ball work because maybe he felt the lads didn't need it – he just wanted to get them fit. His downfall, though, was that many of the lads just didn't take to his ways and personality traits, and that filtered through on a Saturday afternoon, too. The League form suffered and we went on a bad run, but still managed to find our way to the League Cup final against Wolves after seeing Coventry City and Plymouth Argyle off. With a replay in all but one round, it had taken us ten games to get to the final – twice the usual number needed. The final was a bit anti-climactic because nobody seemed to be enjoying themselves the way we used to in the past. We lost to Wolves 2–1, despite a number of good chances, and it was a disappointment to lose because we'd become accustomed to winning those big matches. Plus, we had a forward line of Summerbee, Bell, Lee, Law and Marsh, and should have been too much for a workmanlike Wolves side on the day. Ultimately, that result led to questions being asked about team spirit and the truth was, it was very low.

Dennis Tueart and Mick Horswill signed after the final, with Jeff Clarke going in the other direction to Sunderland, but I played little part in the deals. Many believed that Saunders' time was running out, and the post-final League form was nothing short of abysmal. By Easter, we were beginning to be sucked towards the bottom of the table. We had won one in eight games and Saunders seemed unable to fire the lads up. The atmosphere in the dressing room had reached an all-time low. We were soundly beaten 3–0 by QPR at Loftus Road and, for the board, that was the final straw. Within a few days, Ron had been shown the door at Maine Road. He had headed from Loftus Road straight back to his home in Norwich, from where he was still commuting, while I travelled back to Manchester with the rest of the team to find the chairman was at Piccadilly station, waiting for us. He was looking for Mike Doyle and a few other lads, and I thought it best to call Ron Saunders and tell him something was obviously going down. Ron travelled back to Manchester but, by the time he arrived, it was too late. The decision had been taken to sack him, and that was the end of his brief career as Manchester City boss. He left quietly, and Peter Swales asked me to take on the role as caretaker again, which I was happy to do. We still needed points to stay up, and we earned a great point against reigning champions Liverpool at home and, I believe on the strength of that, I was appointed manager of the club. I'm glad they did it then, because the next game was a 4–0 defeat – to Liverpool again! If they'd delayed it a game, who knows what might have happened? We got a result against West Ham to guarantee our safety, and travelled to Manchester United for the last game of the season.

To avoid relegation, United had to hope that a series of results went their way but, first and foremost, they had to beat us by a cricket score. Denis Law was his usual quiet self in the dressing room before the game, and he was no doubt contemplating a million and one possibilities for the afternoon's action ahead. He, of course, would score the only goal of the game and I was absolutely delighted with the win. I wasn't too fussed with United's relegation, but Denis was distraught afterwards. As far as I was concerned, Denis was a City player – we paid his wages and he had scored a great goal and that was the end of it. In fact, he would never play competitively again in League football. He came to me shortly after to tell me he'd had enough and was quitting, and I could understand that. He'd done a good job for us and that's all I would have asked from him.

The season was over but it was the beginning of my managerial reign. I had the summer to plan next season and had a list of players I had to look at, as well as a few potential targets to consider. I was relishing the role and, as we set off on a pre-season tour of Greece, I felt happy with the way things were going. I was, however, about to have my first dust-up with Peter Swales. I'd taken the lads for a training session and Mr Swales flew in to join the tour. He wasn't happy with the fact I wasn't there to meet him and I told him in no uncertain terms that my place was with the team – not as some half-baked meeter and greeter at the airport.

Around that time, I decided to take on Ian McFarlane as my right-hand man – someone who I'd played alongside at Bath City and someone who I knew would always back my decisions and stand by me. Ian was a good coach and I was aware of his capabilities because he'd done the job at Sheffield Wednesday and Middlesbrough alongside Jack Charlton. I asked Jack if he'd let him join me at City and he agreed to let him go. I knew I could trust him, which was as important to me as any coaching skill.

As for me, the move from player to manager didn't affect me one bit. The relationships with players who had been my teammates may have changed, but it didn't bother me at all. I knew and they knew that, even though I was still the same man, a line had been drawn and that I was on one side and the lads on the other. It's the only way the job can work, because there will be times you have to discipline or omit players and if you're still mates, resentment sets in. Everyone knows a boss isn't there to win a popularity contest, because it won't work. I'd been lucky enough to be given one of the biggest jobs in football and I was going to give it my best shot. I just took a step back and handled it my own way. The job certainly didn't frighten me. In fact, just after I'd been offered the job, I went to see Sir Matt Busby for a bit of advice. He had won everything there was to win in the game and I couldn't think of anyone better to have a quick chat with.

He was a lovely man – a real gentleman, who had been good friends with Joe Mercer, which shows the calibre of friends he attracted. I asked him what advice he could offer me and he said, 'Tony, the job is all about common sense. The only problem is making everyone else see common sense, too!' It was great to see someone with no airs or graces about him, who was as down to earth as you could ever want to be. I kept that advice with me throughout my managerial career.

The biggest problem I now had was to turn things around at the club. Many of the players who had won all the trophies a few years back were still at the club, but they were now the wrong side of 30. Maybe a case of the pot calling the kettle black, you may think, but I needed to start thinking of the future, and that would mean some of the lads, household names or not, would have to go and make way for fresh talent, whether it be from the kids in the reserves or new signings. The thought didn't faze me at all. I knew I would have some problems along the way, but it had to be done.

I had a fair amount of mail from the City fans, congratulating me on my appointment and wishing me well. You'll always have people with you in football who want to see what you are capable of and, because of my role in the team that had won so many trophies, the feeling I got was that they felt I was one of their own – which, of course, I was. If you've got that kind of backing to begin with, plus the support of the dressing room, you're in with a real chance of doing well.

I also knew where I stood with Peter Swales. He never came to me and said that I had x amount of money to spend on new players. He'd either go along with your plans or he wouldn't – simple as that. He'd deal with all the business aspects such as contracts or the finance of transfers, along with club secretary

Bernard Halford, and any terms he could get in the club's favour, he would get. He'd come from a tough business background and was experienced and wily in that respect. I'd learn from the manager of the player I'd be interested in how much they were asking and then go to Mr Swales, who would either say yes or no. There wasn't really much more involved in the transfer process.

TEN

Farewell to the Old Guard

'Tony tends to worry a lot, although having Ian McFarlane around will help take a lot of the load off his shoulders.'

Willie Donachie, 1974

I expected a few knocks on my door once I'd settled into the job and I knew some players would want to test the water and maybe see how I'd react to certain requests or demands. With that in mind, it was Francis Lee who was the first of the big-name players that I had to deal with as manager. Franny had been a tremendous servant to the club and the fans adored him for the key role he'd played in our successes a few years back, but when he walked into my office looking for a substantial pay increase I simply sat down, listened to his request and then his arguments as to why he believed he was worth the extra money. Was he testing me? I can't be certain, but Franny was a shrewd so-and-so when it came to money, so he may well have been seeing how far he could push me. Only he will know the answer to that, however. I took the details down and told him to leave it with me for the time being and I would discuss it with the chairman and see what he had to say.

I never gave him any indication as to how I was feeling about the situation or how I wanted to deal with it. So I had a meeting with Mr Swales and told him that if we were going to agree a new deal with Franny, I'd like it to be based on whether he played or not, and the chairman agreed with me. I wanted to get the best out of him and keep him hungry, because he was a player that thrived on challenges. I went back to Franny and said that we would give him what he was looking for but he would only get the rise when he actually played. If he made an appearance, he'd get paid extra – if not, then he would get his normal basic wage. He was in his 30s now and I was trying to do the right thing by the club and the player to justify the kind of money he was after. There shouldn't have been a problem because he played most games and I picked him when he was fit.

Not entirely unexpectedly, though, Franny wasn't having any of it. Perhaps we'd both gambled and both lost out. I felt he almost certainly had other irons in the fire and had the cushion of knowing that if we didn't give him what he wanted, he would get it elsewhere. I wasn't prepared to bend on the deal and, to my mind, he'd already made his decision to play somewhere else.

Derby County came in shortly after with an acceptable bid for him and I travelled over to the Baseball Ground with Bernard Halford and Franny to meet their people. I was as sure as I could be that he'd been tapped up (spoken to without the club's permission – which happens all the time in football) and was in no doubt that the deal would all go through smoothly. There was an air of disbelief amongst the City fans that we could let someone like Franny go, but I had to do what was best for the club. I had to make changes anyway, and he just happened to be the first.

While Francis Lee headed for the exit door, Asa Hartford was about to become my first signing for City. I knew about him being turned down by Leeds in the past, due to a medical condition, so I sent chief scout Ken Barnes to West Brom to take a look at how things were shaping up for Asa. Ken returned and said, 'Tony, if he's got a hole in his heart, I'll show my arse in Woolworth's front window.' He'd simply judged Asa by his work-rate in the games he'd seen, so I went down to watch him myself and saw the same thing. He had plenty of ability, was a busy and inventive midfielder and I thought he'd make a great signing for the club. We put in a bid of £250,000, which was accepted by Albion, and brought him to Maine Road. He was the type of player I wanted in my side, and it was never a gamble to bring him in. Asa would prove to be one of the best signings I ever made. He was a character, and a ducker and diver, but, first and foremost, he was what I considered to be a Manchester City-type player – plenty of heart with a touch of flair. I claimed to the journalists at the time that he was my 'first piece of gold'.

We prepared for the 1974–75 campaign with Rodney Marsh as the team captain. A few eyebrows may have been raised when I handed him the armband, but I thought the extra responsibility would bring the best out of him. I wanted to make him feel he was wanted and let him know he had a big future in my team. You can never bring a player like Rodney completely into line because that's the way they are – it's part of their make-up. I reckoned if he could play anywhere near his best each week, especially with the talent and flair he possessed, he could really take off.

Elsewhere in the squad, there were still one or two players I really needed to move on. I didn't want to come into the job, make wholesale changes and be crucified for it, so I had to gradually alter the personnel and look of the team. Lawrie McMenemy once told me that if you change things around, do it when it's right for you as the manager, not when it suits the player. It was good advice. When I was about to show someone the door, I never let them know, I just did it quickly. You can get problems when you are dealing with favourites who have been great servants to the club – legends even – because it can fester if it is done over a period of time. It was best for all concerned. That, at least, is what I tried to do, but things wouldn't always be as clear-cut as that.

Something else I was beginning to have to get used to, as a manager, were the very public training sessions we now took at Platt Lane. We'd not long taken over from the police, who used to own the complex on the corner of Platt Lane and Yew Tree Road. It was conveniently placed, a minute from Maine Road, but it was just too open for my liking. Everybody knew what was going on because we always had a fair few punters that came to watch and on a training ground, anything can happen and often does. If somebody went in hard it might end up with the pair involved squaring up to each other, and what should have been private matters were suddenly public property. It was great to have a dedicated complex because we used to have to travel to Cheadle and Urmston when I'd been a player. It did mean, however, there wasn't much point practising elaborate set-piece manoeuvres in case somebody from the opposition had been sent down to size us up. Besides, anything we did work on rarely happened on the pitch, because the lads would invariably do something different during a match.

Then, on 27 November 1974, City awarded me a testimonial, but it turned out to be a disappointing evening on the whole. Don Revie was the England manager at the time, and I was originally hoping he'd bring his team to play City at Maine Road but, for one reason or another, it never came off. So, I was left with the job of trying to scrape a side together to play City and it took a lot of the enjoyment out of the night. The sleet and cold weather didn't help on the night and the gate of 14,598 was not fantastic. It earned me a cheque for £2,500 that, even back then, was not a great deal of money for a testimonial match. I appreciated the support from supporters who had turned out and the lads that played, who included Bobby Charlton, George Best, Frank Lampard and Frank Worthington. Besty had finished at United but made the effort to turn out for my benefit, which I appreciated. It added to the mutual respect between us. The opponents that would have been ideal were, of course, Manchester United. Former Reds' player Bill

Foulkes had a full house for a clash between the two Manchester clubs, as did Alan Oakes, but there just wasn't a date suitable for them to play us – either that or they couldn't forgive my team relegating them the last time we'd met. It was just one of those things.

At home, I would always leave the work back at the club. I never brought it home with me to Sylvia and the kids. I wasn't home that much because I was always somewhere with the club, whether it be training, watching the reserves, supporters club meetings, watching players or any other number of tasks connected with the job. My time at home was precious, and that's how I kept it. My wife and I always enjoyed a Saturday night trip to the Golden Garter in Wythenshawe back then. That was our regular spot, and it gave me a chance to unwind after the games. Tom Jones, Tommy Cooper, Engelbert Humperdinck, Shirley Bassey, Morecambe and Wise and Lovelace Watkins played there, and I've some wonderful memories of the place. We'd get a babysitter – Margaret – to look after the kids and then go and let our hair down. In fact, the kids would keenly ask us when we were going out because Margaret always brought them a big bag of sweets, so they were happy with their end of the deal. To this day, we still go out every Saturday night, even though the kids are grown up and have left home, and the Golden Garter has long since gone. I never had any problems from anyone in the club, even though there were plenty of United fans knocking around. You just had to know how to handle people, and I seemed to do OK and be able to defuse any potential problems.

I was also heavily involved in opening City Supporters Club branches around the country at this point. Peter Swales, Ian Niven, Bernard Halford, Supporters Club chairman Les Saul and his secretary Frank Horrocks and I would pile into two cars and travel around the country – Leicester, Bristol, Nottingham; we went all over the place and it took up quite a bit of time. We'd usually set out on a Thursday evening and go to anywhere where there were

30 or so people who supported Manchester City and wanted to form a supporters club. What we were after at the time was something similar to what went on at United over the years, with fans travelling in groups from all over Britain. If we could get 30 people from Bristol, 40 from Leicester and so on, it might snowball and, to some extent, it did. City have fans all around the UK and the world now, and, thanks to the initiatives of Mr Swales and his board, there are numerous official clubs who make the journey to Manchester for every home game. It certainly opened my eyes to how big City actually were, and if the Bath and Wessex branch (which, incidentally, included my sister-in-law Cora and her husband, John) had anything to do with a number of people back home following my career, then so much the better. The chairman might have got a lot of stick during his career, but his development of the supporters clubs and the Junior Blues have been two of the most significant steps in bringing the club and the supporters closer together, and I feel he deserves a lot of credit for his initiatives.

There were plenty of unsung heroes at Maine Road in those days, and two of them were the laundry women – Janet and Joyce – who washed on average 60 kits a day. This number included the first team and the two youth teams, and sometimes, if we had two training sessions in a day, the workload would be doubled up. Janet and Joyce would wash the kits in these two big washing machines they had, then dry them and have everything ready for the next day. I interviewed one of the girls, Joyce, in 1974 and she only retired from the job in 2004, so I was happy that I made at least one decent long-term signing in all that time . . . These are the types of people that make a club tick and never receive any credit for what they do. I used to take them a tipple along every Friday as a small thank you and they would enjoy their brandy and lemonade before getting back to work again.

Then there were the commissionaires – uniformed officers who had mostly retired and seen some service. They used to be our security on match days, and there were a few characters amongst these lads, too. Malcolm used to wind a few of them up by leaving tickets for some of his guests with 'Lady or Lord so-and-so' on the envelope. When they called at Maine Road to pick them up from the front door, the commissionaires would bow to the bogus dignitaries as they got out!

We began the new season well, and big Ian McFarlane was doing a great job as my number two. He was popular with the lads because he liked a laugh and a joke, but they all respected him and worked hard on the training pitch for him. We had a good run of results at the start of the season and were up at the top early on after beating Liverpool 2–0. We had a bit of a sticky patch after that but we were holding our own. I recall Rodney Marsh scoring a fantastic overhead kick against QPR, but it was no real surprise for us because we all knew that he was capable of it – he'd do it every other day in training at Platt Lane. Rodney had an abundance of talent, and it was all about finding the best way to get all that ability out of him. He liked his freedom and was always challenging things. He was outspoken, and that's just the type of player he was. I did everything I could for the lad while he was at City to help him be a success at the club.

There were mornings when he was late for training, usually along with Mickey Horswill, who was a single lad who had a smart apartment, so when they were missing I'd pick up the phone and say, 'Get your arses in training!' to either Mick or Rod. I did that a few times, but I shouldn't really have ever had to do it. I thought that as long as they turned up, though, I could get them at it. I'd give them a rollicking and send them out with the rest of the lads, but around the third time I did it, I realised it just wasn't going to work out. The real problems with Rodney, however, were only just beginning.

Back in the League, Franny was back at Maine Road with Derby County and, knowing Francis as I did, he no doubt had a point to prove. There were no hard feelings so far as I was concerned, but the way football works is that there are always players who will come back and haunt you and that's exactly what happened in this match. There's not much you can do about it – you've just got to be big enough to take it on the chin. So, when Franny picked up the ball 25 yards out, looked up and struck a cracking drive into the top corner, it didn't surprise me because I'd seen him do it so many times before. He was a great player and, given the space and time (which he had been on this occasion), he'd hurt you. We lost that game on the back of a 4–1 defeat at Liverpool, so it wasn't the best of weeks.

Meanwhile, we were interested in bringing Joe Royle to the club and put in a bid to Everton, which they accepted. We'd watched him a few times because we needed a target man and Joe fitted the bill perfectly. I saw him as the perfect player to add a bit of muscle to the forward line and he would go on to do a great job for me. The season trundled on and Colin Bell and Dennis Tueart were scoring goals for us. I'd also brought young 18-year-old winger Peter Barnes, who was showing a lot of promise, into the side. You had to get the ball to him because he could turn defenders inside out, but the game was changing at the time, in that the systems most teams were playing were 4–4–2. There would be two wide midfielders, who would also track back and tackle, but Peter wouldn't do that – he just wasn't made to mark and tackle. Going forward, he was a different prospect. I played him because I thought we could get away with it, and he did really well for us on the whole.

In defence, I brought in Jeff Hammond from Ipswich because we were struggling for a full-back. He was a solid defender who did well during his stay but, ultimately, he didn't play too many games for us. In goal, I recalled Joe Corrigan to the first team at the start of the season. Johnny Hart had signed Keith MacRae as the new number one, because Joe had been struggling with weight, form and confidence. Keith did quite well, but I knew if I could get Joe going again, he would do even better for us. He worked hard for me in training and I felt he deserved another crack. Once he got back in, he was there for good. That was what I wanted from players – determination and desire. It was a hard decision to drop Keith but I had to do what I felt was best for the club. I remember Dennis Tueart picking up an injury and I didn't recall him when he was fit again because the team was doing well. He wasn't best pleased, and told me in no uncertain terms that he felt he should be back in the side, but I said that he'd have to wait until he was selected again. I didn't mind his attitude because I wanted players who believed in themselves and were desperate to play – they didn't get their own way, but it showed passion for the shirt, which is all you could ask for as a manager.

We finished my first full season in eighth position in the League and I had to be happy with that. We'd changed a few things around and I was shaping the side more in the way I believed it should be, but there was still some pruning to do in the squad and still some big names to move on. One of them was my old mate from the West Country, Mike Summerbee. As I stated earlier, when I felt the time was right for a player to move on, I tried to do things as quickly as I could, and Mike's case was no exception.

Mike was a legend at the club and had been a brilliant player, but it couldn't carry on forever. He'd have been the first to admit he wasn't the player he had been because age was catching up with him and, when Burnley came in with an offer, I said I was happy for him to have a chat with them. I talked the move over with him and he agreed it was perhaps time to move on. The deal suited everyone and, though it was the end of another fantastic era, it had to happen. Mike knew I was planning changes and I'd be lying if I said the situation wasn't a little uncomfortable, but it was my job to make awkward decisions.

The 1974–75 season hadn't been a spectacular start to my managerial career but we'd finished in a steady eighth position. This was an improvement of six places on the previous year, but nowhere near what I was after. Derby County had won the League and so Franny's decision to move to the Rams had been fully vindicated. He became one of a select few for picking up two championship medals at two different clubs.

With the season just finished, we set off on an end-of-season tour to Nigeria: not the best of destinations for an English football team, but the organisers had thrown in a five-day break in Madeira to entice us. Nigeria was a frightening place, however. We arrived at the airport and got on a bus for the hotel and, a short way into the journey, we saw someone who had been knocked down and just left for dead at the side of the road. It seemed that no one was particularly bothered about his misfortune, and the bus just moved on without any of us knowing whether he would pull through, or had died where he lay – not a great first impression of the country. The hotel wasn't brilliant but the food was OK, and the games were a good workout for the lads. What sticks in my mind is Joe Corrigan running out of his room in terror after he'd seen what he thought was a rat run across the top of his curtains! I was in stitches that the big fella was so shook up about it and I wondered if he had dreamt it. Either way, he wouldn't go back in that room and I can't say I blamed him, either.

We won both tour games by a single goal against two physically tough sides named Shooting Stars and Nigerian Forces. They were both military-based so they had a high level of fitness and were obviously used to the conditions. We had a golf day but their greens were actually sand and tar, which stirred up a few memories of my time in India. The people were good to us but there were guards constantly shadowing our every move, so we could sense that the country was perhaps a little unstable. It was hot and humid but, considering the sticky conditions, I was pleased to win the games and even happier to head back for our short holiday in Madeira.

There was another new face for the 1975–76 season, with the arrival of Dave Watson from Sunderland. Ian McFarlane had recommended Dave to me and I checked him out for myself as soon as I had the chance. I didn't need a second look because he was a quality defender who I reckoned could forge a great partnership with Mike Doyle. Tommy Booth had been struggling with a back injury for a while and I had to get somebody else in as cover. Kenny Clements had also broken into the team and was a promising full-back, so we'd assembled a great mix of youth and experience on the playing staff.

Another player Ian recommended could have been a tremendous asset to the team – had he not already been promised to Liverpool. We made a move for Graeme Souness whilst he was at Middlesbrough, but the Anfield club had already spoken to him and he'd supposedly verbally agreed to join them. Ian had become close to Souness whilst he was at Middlesbrough, and thought he'd be just the type of player we needed – a born winner and a natural leader – but we just missed out on bringing him to Maine Road.

We started the season well, but, just as we had the previous year, we hit a blip on our away form. For one reason or another, we just couldn't buy a win away from Maine Road. We tried a few variations on away trips, but I didn't believe it would really make much difference because I reckoned it was down to the players and their approach to the matches. No amount of tinkering with the routine was going to make any difference to that. One game at Norwich caused the Canaries boss, John Bond, to have a go at my side in the press. We'd ground out a draw in the League Cup and he obviously felt aggrieved that his team had missed their chance. He claimed we'd gone there with a negative attitude, and in the replay at Maine Road they managed to hold us to a 2–2 draw. In the second replay, we turned in a hell of a display and beat them 6–1 at Stamford Bridge. We didn't hear too much from Bondy about negativity after that! Brian Clough claimed he was glad City had won through because he wanted to face the best team in the next round. He'd left Derby and, via Brighton and Leeds, had now become manager of the Rams' deadly rivals – and he was without doubt the best manager around at the time. He was in a league of his own when it came to dealing with the media, supporters and, of course, the players. I really liked him and he would invariably give me a peck on the cheek whenever he saw me! Only he could get away with that, and I had such a lot of respect for him that I was happy to lock horns with his team in the next round. We were still trundling along nicely, but the situation with Rodney Marsh was about to explode. Our first win on the road came, in all places, at Arsenal – one of our traditional graveyards. We beat them 3–2 at Highbury, and that was to be Rodney's last game in City's colours.

I'd made up my mind that I could live without him because I felt we could only carry one flair player and we had enough of those in the team to let him go. He would give you the odd flash of brilliance and then go missing for large periods of the game and, with young Barnes in the side now, I no longer felt we could carry Marsh as well. The punters loved him and I knew I would get a lot of stick for shipping him out, which is exactly what happened. There were a lot of letters, graffiti and all kinds of things going on. One said, 'Book out, Marsh in!' on a wall across from my office at Maine Road – the writing was literally on the wall for Rodney now! But none of it made any difference, because I'd made the decision not to play him again and I wasn't going to change my mind. I waited to see if any offers would come in for Rodney but they never did, which caused a few problems. He trained with the first team and played for the reserves and we had a few little run-ins along the way, but nothing too dramatic.

I was never a great smiler as such and he turned up for training one day with a T-shirt on just saying 'Smile'. I knew what he was trying to do so I let it ride and I went out and got a T-shirt of my own which had 'Play' written on it. I wore it the next day and it conveyed more than anything I could have said at the time. There was a bit of cat and mouse going on but it wasn't going to change anything regarding his future with the club. I made Mike Doyle, who was having a great season, the skipper, and he was undoubtedly the right man for the job. He was a local kid who I felt would rally the lads around, and he also had the backing of his teammates, which was hugely important.

Back in the League Cup, we saw off Nottingham Forest 2–1 at Maine Road and were drawn at home to Manchester United in the last 16. It was to be the game in which we lost the services of Colin Bell for a considerable period of time, as he sustained a terrible injury against United. The one thing that sticks in my mind about that night was that Colin was running in a straight line, and if he had carried on running in the same direction, he would have been fine. Unfortunately, he checked to come inside and Martin Buchan stuck a leg out, caught his knee and he went down in a heap. The first thing I thought was that I hoped it was just a knock and we could get him patched up for the rest of the game. But he stayed down – something he'd never done before – so I knew it was serious. I didn't know just how bad it was until the end of the match, when physio Freddie Griffiths gave me a full report. I still didn't think it would be anywhere near as severe as it turned out to be.

I saw him after the match and I could see in his face how much pain he was in. His knee was already beginning to bruise and swell. I was devastated for the lad because he was a magnificent player and our most consistent performer. His injury cast a black cloud over the club for a while because he was simply irreplaceable.

This gave Paul Power a chance to break into the team, and he formed a midfield with Alan Oakes, Asa Hartford and Peter Barnes. Paul gave us the work-rate without the all-round ability of Colin and he did well, to be fair to him. We were lucky in that respect, because it could have affected us terribly if we'd had someone come in who wasn't up to the job, and any new signing was obviously in an unfavourable position compared to Colin. We saw United off 4–0 that night and started to think of Wembley when we pulled Mansfield Town out of the hat for the quarter-finals. We beat them 4–2, but they gave us a good game with Asa finishing them off in the last minute. We always felt at that time that, even if we conceded goals, we could score more than our opponents.

We were paired with Middlesbrough in the semi-final, to be played over two legs. We knew they'd be tough nuts to crack on their own ground, but we'd already seen them off 4–0 at Maine Road a couple of months earlier so we were quietly confident. Ironically, we would play them in the League three days before, too.

We saw off Hartlepool 6–0 in the FA Cup third round but, away from the knockout competitions, Middlesbrough struck a psychological blow by beating us 1–0 in the League, three days before the semi-final. I've lost count as to the number of times you meet the same opponents twice-running in the League and Cup, but we weren't too downhearted because we should have left Ayresome Park with at least a draw and we hadn't seen anything to make us unduly concerned about their attack.

We travelled back to Cleveland a few days later for the first leg and, again, lost by a single goal on the night. That didn't set us up too badly for the return and we repeated the dose we'd given 'Boro earlier in the season. I remember there was a fantastic atmosphere inside Maine Road that night. There were 44,426 people packed in and Alan Oakes gave us the best possible start with one of his left-foot specials within the first five minutes. I'd also put young Ged Keegan in the team after a handful of games the previous season and he made it 2–0 after just 11 minutes' play. We'd raced out of the blocks and were playing some cracking stuff. We went on to win 4–0 and booked a place at Wembley against Newcastle United.

It was a great achievement for the team and we'd proven ourselves to be a great cup team yet again. As manager, I was obviously delighted to be in a major final in only my second full season. I took the team away, prior to the February final, for a bit of rest and relaxation. We went to a health farm at Tring in Hertfordshire for four days, and Dave Watson was struggling to be fit for the weekend. He had a chronic back problem and was forced to sleep on the floor for three nights to ease the pain. He was a vital member of my starting eleven and, with Malcolm Macdonald still firing on all cylinders for Newcastle, I desperately needed him to be fit. The rest of the lads loved the physiotherapy and pampering so the build-up was perfect. I'd made my mind up for the final team and had decided to keep the side that had seen off Middlesbrough in the semi-final.

Ged Keegan had done really well since coming in and, with Kenny Clements out injured, I put him in at right-back. I had no special plans for marking Macdonald – I just let Dave Watson, who had just about passed a fitness test, and Mike Doyle sort it out between them. Doyley picked him up, as it happened, and did a fantastic job that I believe convinced Don Revie to give him his first England cap. It was totally different leading the side out at Wembley Stadium in a suit, when all I'd been used to was running out as captain. It still felt great but if the fact that I'd hung my boots up hadn't completely sunk in up to that moment, it did the minute I stepped out onto the pitch with the lads behind me. We stuck Ian McFarlane on at the back of the lads as a reward for all his efforts, and I think it was a moment he'll never forget. The game itself was memorable for lots of reasons but the goals will always stick in my mind more than anything else. We'd worked on a couple of set-piece routines in training and, in the end, they turned out to be the main reasons we won the game.

We had a chance to put our hard work into action when we were awarded a free kick midway in the Newcastle half. The ball was floated in and Mike Doyle pulled away to the back post, whilst decoys ran in the other direction. Doyley, with space and time, headed the ball back across the box for Peter Barnes to volley the ball into the net. Alan Gowling pulled the Geordies level, but Dennis Tueart scored that incredible overhead kick to win it for us. He'd had a fairly quiet game up to that point, too, but he came up with something special and scored the kind of winner all kids dream of. It was a great result and I remember looking up in the stands at the chairman Peter Swales and seeing the elation on his face. He'd wanted this as bad as anyone else and I was as happy for him as I was for anybody. The City fans were fantastic but they had become used to winning at Wembley. I was later informed that I had become the first person to win the League Cup as a player and a manager. At that time, nobody imagined it would be the last trophy we won for almost 30 years but that's the way it's turned out. I'm sure that particular run won't continue for too much longer.

There was a downside to the day, however, and that was due to the loss of my right-hand man, Ian McFarlane, as coach. Ian had a house in Middlesbrough and he'd taken out a bridging loan to buy a house in Sale. He came to me to say that it was now costing him a lot of money, and asked if I thought the board could help him. I said I would arrange a meeting for him with the directors but the rest was up to him. I backed him as much as I could but, ultimately, he had to fight his own corner. He went to see them and asked if they could buy his house in Cleveland so he could get rid of the bridging loan. The club considered his request but refused to help. From that moment on, he was always going to leave City. He was a dogged and stubborn Scot and he told them if they weren't prepared to help, then he didn't want to stay any longer. I knew the likely outcome because he'd already told me as much, and there wasn't anything I could do to stop him going. It was a real pity because he had a great relationship with the players and we'd just won our first trophy as a team, so we were really on our way. But he had his principles. The bottom line, as far as I was concerned, was that I needed to find a new coach. Meanwhile, I had to get on with managing the club and keeping the squad in peak condition.

With Colin Bell's future in doubt, we had a chance to sign Arsenal midfielder Alan Ball. His father had got in touch with me to say that his son wanted to return north and was available for the right price. I was really interested because I knew what a good player he was. I put it to the board and also informed them that the player wanted a house chucked in as part of the deal. I didn't think that was a problem at the time, but one of the directors at the board meeting was fairly negative about the whole deal. He was obviously against him joining the club. He aired his views, and when it came to the vote it went in favour of not signing the player. I accepted it because it was part and parcel of the management game. I'd done all I could but got a knock-back on this particular occasion. I knew that the chairman gave the directors a mandate to say their piece and at each board meeting there would be a couple of them who had been, shall we say, primed to ask me questions. Swales was a businessman and hard as nails when he needed to be, but I think he liked it if others occasionally put the spanner in the works so he didn't come out of it all looking like the bad guy. I knew what was going on and that was good enough for me.

All this time I was being kept up-to-date on Colin's progress by the club surgeon, Sydney Rose, but the odds were stacked against him returning. Colin worked so hard all the time to try and regain his fitness. I was desperate for the lad to succeed – not just for the club's sake, but because he deserved it. I'd see him going in the gym or doing some leg-work in the stands, enduring some discomfort as he focused on the day he could pull that blue jersey on again. I've never seen anyone who worked harder than Colin in all my years in football. The trouble was, every time he took one step forward, he had some kind of a knock that put him back to square one again, so we all knew it wasn't going to be easy for him to get back. It was a long, hard and lonely road for him.

ELEVEN

The Second-best Team in England

'I owe it all to Tony Book. He had faith in me and despite my poor start, he never lost it.'

Joe Royle, 1976

My second full season in charge had seen us end in eighth position for the second successive season. We'd won the League Cup, but I was looking to improve on our final League standing for the coming season because we were capable of much more than just a top ten finish. We ended the 1975–76 campaign with a tour to Japan and South Korea and it proved to be a great trip for all the lads, most of whom had never been to East Asia before. There was plenty of travelling involved and no shortage of excitement on the pitch because the games were competitive and the crowds lively.

The military were always present and there was one time when Asa Hartford and Dennis Tueart were involved in a bust-up on the pitch in one of the games. I half-expected the guards would run and open fire on our lads! Thankfully, they didn't, but it kept you on edge having armed chaperones watching our every move.

We beat the Japanese national side four times and South Korea in two games out of three. The crowds were colourful and averaged about 10,000, but the games became a bit monotonous because we were playing the same teams in three or four successive games. It was while we were out there that Asa had a close escape that could have easily gone horribly wrong. I think he just had a towel on in a hotel room and, if I recall correctly, a supporter had called for an autograph. He walked towards the door and ended up walking through a plate glass door, which broke and smashed in on him. It was incredible that he wasn't hurt and escaped with no more than a little cut.

We were in East Asia for just under three weeks and it was nice to get back home and put our feet up for five minutes – which, incidentally, is all I felt I had.

I needed to get busy in the transfer market and had targeted Brian Kidd – who was great pals with Mike Doyle and also a Manchester lad – as a player I wanted on board. Kiddo was a quality player and I'd heard he wanted to leave Arsenal and return to the Manchester area. I knew he'd score goals for us and I also knew he was a good lad to have in the dressing room. He could get others going with his enthusiasm and that would carry over and spread throughout the team. He could handle himself, too. It was a fairly straightforward deal because he was keen to join City and we had no trouble agreeing a fee of £100,000 with Arsenal.

Another new arrival was that of first-team coach Bill Taylor. I got in touch with Don Revie and told him I was looking for a top man and he suggested Bill, who was then at Fulham and also coaching England. I approached Fulham and they gave me permission to speak with him. We met and I instantly liked him and offered him the job, which, happily, he accepted. He was completely different to Ian McFarlane – much quieter but with a nice way about him. His training methods were first class and, most importantly, the players took to him straight away.

I also brought in Jimmy Conway from Fulham, shortly after Kiddo's arrival. He was recommended by Bill and with Colin's situation ongoing, I felt I needed a bit more strength in depth and signing Jimmy seemed a logical step to take. He rarely gave the ball away and was a good, honest footballer. He was the last signing of the summer and I now felt I had a side that could have a real go at the championship. Consistency would be the key and if we could cure our away sickness, we'd be in with a real chance of challenging Liverpool. One player who wouldn't be with us for the new campaign was Alan Oakes, who left for Chester. Alan had given the club fantastic service, but we both knew the time had come for him to move on. He lived near Chester so the move made sense for Alan and for us. Later in the season, Maine Road was full for his testimonial against Manchester United as the fans showed their appreciation of one of their all-time greats. I would have kept him on the coaching staff but he wanted to keep playing and I could certainly appreciate that. He'd been worth his weight in gold for the Blues and was a great lad, too: someone you could always rely on to give you everything every time he played. He would be hard to replace.

Around this time, we were the subjects of a season-long section on the BBC TV evening magazine show *Nationwide*. The cameras were given access to all areas as they covered the day-to-day running of the club and featured it in a segment called 'Saturday's Heroes'. To be honest, it was a difficult time for us because it felt like an intrusion in many ways. It was the first time anything like that had been done and I suppose it was good PR for the club. The chairman, who had no doubt struck up a profitable deal to allow the cameras *carte blanche* was all for it but, for the rest of us, it was a bit uncomfortable having a camera shoved in your face every day. We went along with it, all the same, because we had no other choice. As a manager, every little incident was now under the scrutiny of a camera crew and, by the time they packed up for the last time, I was glad to see the back of them. One good thing was that the lads were so used to being on television that whenever Granada or the BBC filmed our games, our lads never became overawed by the coverage.

The squad was looking good, with a sound defence, strong midfield and an experienced forward line. All in all, I'd added Royle, Kidd, Watson, Hartford and Conway and we had emerging talent such as Gary Owen, Barnes, Clements, Power and Ged Keegan. The right-back berth was still something of a problem and I brought in Mick Docherty, son of Manchester United boss Tommy, to start in the new season and give us a bit of cover in that area. We looked a useful team and I was especially pleased with the fact that we kept 9 clean sheets out of the first 15 League games. It had to be right in defence if we were going to sustain a challenge at the top. After just 5 League wins in my first 44 away games as manager, we'd finally begun to pick up points on our travels, but still only won two of the first nine games that campaign, drawing six and losing once – we'd also drawn one third of our opening 15 matches 0–0.

Mike Doyle and Dave Watson were outstanding, and Kenny Clements and Willie Donachie were doing a fine job as full-backs. Big Joe was in the kind of form that made him an England squad regular and our solidity at Maine Road was as impressive as ever. Too many draws, though, were a cause for concern and by the end of the year we'd drawn half of our games. While the League form was good, we went out of the League Cup at the first hurdle, 3–0 to Aston Villa, so there would be no defending the crown on this occasion. In the UEFA Cup, we'd been handed one of the toughest pairings in the competition – Juventus. They had a team packed with Italian internationals and we would have to beat the favourites to win the Cup in the first round if we were to progress.

We went and had a look at them in Turin to see what system they played, but I'd never been one to worry too much about the opposition. I always thought if your team played well enough the opposition would have enough problems of their own. Juventus had a team of great players and at least three or four that could really hurt you, given the chance. The first leg at Maine Road was a tight, mean match. They had some tough characters and played hard, controlled football. They were one of the great Italian sides of that era and we just edged it 1–0 with a goal from Kidd. The crowd were magnificent that night and it was a great European football night in Manchester – the sort I believed the club should be having far more often than they were.

The second leg was always going to be extremely tough, especially going into the match on the back of a 3–1 home defeat to Manchester United – not the best preparation for such a crucial game. Juventus scored an early goal to put us on the back foot straight away and, with 55,000 fans urging them on, they added a killer second to take the game 2–1 on aggregate. There was no disgrace in being put out by Juventus and they went on to win the competition, as if further proof was needed that we'd faced the best side. It was just bad luck on our part, because I feel we could have gone all the way had we avoided them.

We picked up our League form again and, with Joe Corrigan in the form of his life and a settled back four, we were one of the hardest teams to beat. Up to Christmas, we'd lost just once at home and once away. We were neck and neck at the top of the table and on 29 December we faced Liverpool, our main rivals, at home. More than 50,000 crammed into Maine Road to see Joe Royle put us 1–0 up on a rock-hard, frosty pitch. As daylight faded, the ground became more treacherous and, with minutes to go, a cross came in and Dave Watson lost his footing. He ended up putting the ball over his own goalkeeper, who was helpless to stop it, and earned Liverpool a crucial point. Little did we know just how costly that lost point would become at the end of the season.

We followed that up with three successive League wins and progressed to the FA Cup fifth round after victories at West Brom and Newcastle. We plugged on, but lost three out of four games – at Old Trafford, Bristol City and also in the FA Cup at Leeds. That pegged us back quite a bit and we travelled to Anfield for a showdown with Liverpool in April, knowing we had to come away with something. We ultimately lost 2–1, though. With eight games to go we knew we couldn't afford any more slip-ups. We won our next three games before facing Derby County at the Baseball Ground. There was hardly a blade of grass left on the pitch, and we saved our worst performance for the worst possible time and were thrashed 4–0. It was just a bad day at the office, but it left us with a mountain to climb. A point at Villa Park hardly helped the cause, but we at least turned on the style to beat Tottenham 5–0. The championship was all but over now, and a draw at home to Everton confirmed as much. We beat Coventry on the last day 1–0, to finish the campaign a point behind the winners – Liverpool – wondering what might have been, but knowing we'd given them a bloody good run for their money.

Peter Swales announced in the close season that he was rewarding me with a new three-year contract worth £25,000 a year. It wouldn't make a great deal of difference to my lifestyle, and represented about a £5,000 raise. I always felt I was underpaid at City, simply because I'd come through the ranks at the club. It's a different ball game if a club wants you to come and manage them because you can pretty much, within reason, name your price. Still, it represented some security for my family.

We began the 1977–78 season believing that we could go one better this time, and had added England striker Mick Channon to the squad. I'd heard he was available thanks to Peter Swales' and Bill Taylor's England connections, and he cost us £300,000 from Southampton. I hoped his attacking flair down the right wing just might be the final piece of the jigsaw and the fee, a record for the club at the time, showed that the board were willing to back my judgement. Mick was a West Country lad like me and was a good, solid pro. I got along well with him but things didn't really go that well for Mick at City and we never really saw the kind of form he'd shown at The Dell. It's always a danger when someone has been at another club for so long, but there's no way of knowing whether it will work out.

Mick's arrival was the beginning of the end for Joe Royle. We had Brian Kidd, Dennis Tueart and now Channon, and places up front were going to be at a premium. I felt that if any two of the strikers I had could hit 20 goals in a season, we'd finish somewhere in the top three. I had no preconceived plan to get rid of Joe but, as the season went along, it seemed right to move him on. Our first-round UEFA Cup exit didn't help matters – we dipped out to Widzew Lodz on away goals, despite leading 2–0 at Maine Road with not long left. Their star midfielder, Boniek, was magnificent for the Poles that night and inspired them to recover to a 2–2 draw. Despite a brave enough effort from us in the return, Lodz sat back and just defended their away goals and went through after a 0–0 draw. Europe was proving a bit of a stumbling block for us, and we just didn't seem to be learning anything from our early exits. The local press claimed the exit was a disgrace, as Lodz were unknown and should have been easily dispatched, but they were a good side and were not dissimilar to the Polish side Groclin, who the Blues lost out to in 2003.

One of the Man City directors, Simon Cousins, wrote me a four-page essay on where he felt the team was going wrong when playing away from home, but I took one glance at it, tore it up and threw it in the bin.

I can recall having a home match somewhere around this time, shortly after one of our European trips, and there was a fair amount of snow that had fallen prior to the next League game at Maine Road. I knew the lads were tired and we had one or two players doubtful for the game so I went out onto the pitch with Stan Gibson. Maine Road was under a blanket of snow but if it had been cleared, we could have got the pitch playable, especially with our excellent under-soil heating system. I decided it would be more beneficial for the team if we could get the match called off, so I said to Stan that I thought we should try to get the game cancelled and asked him to water it all over and make the conditions icy as well. The sub-zero temperatures soon froze the surface water and by the time the referee arrived, it was totally unplayable, and the official agreed as much. The games had been coming one after another with no break in-between, so I didn't feel any guilt and I'm positive that similar situations arose at other clubs from time to time. It was the only occasion I've played a part in helping a match to be postponed but with snow and ice surrounding the ground and terraces, too, maybe it was the best thing all round.

Joe Royle played his last game in a 3–1 win over Liverpool in October 1977, joining Bristol City, initially on loan, shortly after. In fact, Joe scored four on his debut for Bristol and would later play for Norwich City. He was a lovely lad – as I've said before – but he was a gentle giant who was just lacking a bit of devilment that would have made him an even better player. Joe had accepted that the move away from Maine Road had become inevitable and we parted on very good terms.

Jim Conway had left in the close season after just one season with us. Jim's one fault was that he lacked a bit of pace and I needed someone who got forward and back quickly. We had begun the new campaign well and believed we could win the championship so long as we were consistent all season. Peter Barnes, Gary Owen and Paul Power were all reaching their peak and Dennis Tueart was on fire up front. We were unbeaten for the first eight League games, taking thirteen points out of a possible sixteen. The first reverse was at Coventry City, where we lost 4–2 and, despite beating Arsenal 2–1 at home four days later, we went into the first of two sizeable blips that would eventually cost us any chance of the title. Four defeats either side of a 3–1 win over champions Liverpool would always give us a lot to do, but we believed there was still a fair way to go.

Our form was excellent, but Nottingham Forest's was exceptional. They were the team to catch, under the stewardship of the brilliant Brian Clough, who reminded me a lot of Malcolm in that he'd had to quit playing well before his time and had gone on to excel in coaching and management. His team was a hard-working, solid outfit who gave everything for their manager. They beat us 2–1 at the City ground and really were a top-class outfit who had two former City players playing out of their skin in the side, too. Ian Bowyer and Colin Barrett both enjoyed the kind of success with Forest that neither player had really had the chance of at Maine Road. Ian was a lovely lad who I had a lot of time for, and we still keep in touch to this day. He'd been forced to leave City because the crowd had turned on him, and he showed a lot of character to fight his way through that period and flourish with his next club. There was also the chance that I held an ace or two up my sleeve for the second half of the season. I'd been monitoring Colin Bell's progress and he was definitely getting somewhere near to being able to play football again. His bravery and determination deserved to be rewarded, and I felt that, even if he wasn't firing on all cylinders, he was still a great asset to have in or around the team.

It was Boxing Day, 1977 against Newcastle that Colin finally made his long-awaited comeback and it's a day anyone who was in the 45,811 Maine Road crowd will never forget. We were locked 0–0 at half-time and, before the team talk, I turned to Colin and said, 'Get yourself ready, you're coming on now.' It was fairly quiet and I think the other players were waiting for this moment, too. I felt a bit emotional when I told him, because not only did it represent the end of a long road to save his career, I also knew what was coming from the City fans.

I sent the team out and followed them down the tunnel. Halfway down, I stopped and listened to the roar. It was amazing. I recall the kids hanging over the tunnel and it began with them shouting, 'It's him!', and from there it went around the ground. There then followed an incredible ovation that would have melted even the hardest of hearts. The City fans' favourite son had returned. The buzz lifted the rest of the team and we ran out 4–0 winners, with Dennis Tueart haunting his boyhood heroes once again with a stunning hat-trick – his second in four years against them at Maine Road. Everyone believed we'd take off again now that Colin was back – such was his aura. It was – and still is – an amazing relationship between Colin and the fans.

It did give us a tremendous boost – more than I'd dared to imagine, in fact. Including the win over Newcastle, we won seven straight League games to battle it out with Liverpool and Nottingham Forest at the top. Going into March, we still had an outside chance of becoming champions but an incredibly timed bad run of one win in eight games – five of which were draws – left us with an impossible task. Nottingham Forest had opened up a massive gap at the top, and even if we'd won all our final five games, we couldn't have caught them. We managed only two wins to end in fourth place. We'd qualified for Europe again, but it felt like we'd failed, somehow. But for those two long bad runs, we'd have probably given Forest a closer run. In theory, we could easily have won the title two years running and I will always maintain that had Glyn Pardoe and Colin Bell not suffered the long-term injuries that they did, City would have gone on to win many more trophies. They were two very good, fit players who meant so much to the team, but alas, we'll never know.

A great era was about to end at the club, and nothing epitomised this better than the departure of Mike Doyle, who was the last of the lads with whom I'd enjoyed the bulk of the glory days. He was captain of the team and a good leader, and, again, I think if he'd been fit for the whole of the '77–78 season, it would have helped us enormously in our quest for the championship. At 29 years old, he still had a lot to offer, but a series of injuries had restricted his appearances. Mike was a true dyed in the wool Blue. He knew when it was time to move on, though, and when Stoke City came in with a bid, I did all I could to help him achieve the move. In the end, he left for £50,000 and he did very well for Stoke. There were no hard feelings from Mike about the move – he wasn't that type of lad.

TWELVE

The Ones That Got Away

Around the 1977–78 season, the club's wage bill began rocketing and I blamed the number of England internationals on City's books for that. We had the likes of Joe Corrigan, Peter Barnes, Dennis Tueart, Mick Channon and Dave Watson, and I used to hate it when England played because it would always cause problems for me. The players would meet other lads from other clubs whilst preparing for an international match and invariably compare wages. If the City player was on less, he'd come to me on his return and ask for more money. If someone was on £200 and they felt somebody of a similar position was on £250 they would come in and ask for more. It happened several times and I grew to hate our lads being called up for England . . . I'd take their request to the chairman and, because he was a senior FA member, he would know there was little he could do but approve the rise. He saw what happened first hand on these occasions and it was the same at all the clubs. There was not much you could do except give them what they wanted or say they could leave if they weren't happy, and who wants to lose their best players? I even got a call once from Penny Watson, wife of Dave Watson, berating me for having her husband in the day after an England game. I informed her that City paid his wages and Thursday training was a normal practice for everyone.

Having said that, her husband was the captain now Doyley had gone and, although I approached the 1978–79 season with a feeling of business as usual, things were beginning to change behind the scenes. It wouldn't be apparent for a few months but, as the season moved on, all kinds of things were happening around me. I'd watched the 1978 World Cup, like everyone else, with great interest and there were several players I would have loved to bring to Maine Road. One in particular was Polish captain Kaziu Deyna. Bill Taylor had seen him at close quarters and thought he'd be a tremendous asset for the club. I travelled over to Poland after the World Cup with secretary Bernard Halford and we met with representatives from Kaziu's club to iron out the finer points of the deal. Part of the payment included sending photocopying machines and other hardware over to them. They weren't that bothered about cash, just stuff they couldn't readily get hold of in Poland. The language barrier was difficult, but there was a lad from our club who had travelled with us and could speak Polish, and his help was invaluable.

So we completed the deal and then we had to get Kaziu and his family to Manchester and get them settled in. We had to take them around the shops and buy them practically everything they needed to set up home. It was a difficult period for all concerned, but he was a class player with a lot of ability so we thought it was well worth all the extra trouble. Red tape and dealing with the Polish Army as well as his club Legia Warsaw meant that it was late November before he was finally ready to make his League debut for City. But, as with a lot of foreign players, he found it hard to adjust to the physical demands of not only the game over here, but the training, too, and he was a past master at ducking out of training.

We used to do a running session at Wythenshawe Park on a Monday morning and he used to come first thing and go straight to see the physio, Roy Bailey. I always knew in advance who was carrying a knock from the weekend match, but Kaziu's ailments always developed over Sunday night! Roy would call me and say, 'He's in again,' with a tight hamstring or suchlike and all I could do was tell him to look after him while we headed out to training. Of course, when I got back to Maine Road, the 'injured' Kaziu was in the gym playing head tennis. That was his mentality – if he had the ball, he was happy, but as for the physical side of football, he didn't really want to know. It has to be said that a lot of foreign players I've come into contact with since have had similar attitudes.

There were some games he played when he was different class and I wouldn't have expected any less from him. But the problems began to outweigh what he was doing out on the pitch. He would occasionally go missing and we'd find him in the Polish Club up at Cheetham Hill, which was obviously because he was missing home and wanted to be around his own people, but we managed to sort that out. I discovered that Kaziu would understand what he wanted to understand and nothing more. There would be times I would try to explain something to him and he would shrug and say 'No understand, no understand,' but I could use the same language for something more favourable to him and he understood perfectly well.

If he was an enigma wrapped in a mystery, he could always answer his critics out on the park, and he did just that on the occasions he played. The problem for me, though, was that he only managed eleven starts in his first season, scoring six goals in the last six games of the season.

Another player with international pedigree I was interested in bringing to Maine Road would have caused a sensation if I could have managed to pull the deal off. Kevin Keegan was coming to the end of his time at SV Hamburg after three wonderful years in Germany and two European Player of the Year awards. There wasn't a manager in England who wouldn't have loved to have had Keegan in their team but, sadly for us, he opted for Southampton instead of coming to Maine Road. I think that had a lot to do with his relationship with Lawrie McMenemy, and I can only imagine the effect he could have had on the fans, and how sensational the team would have been with him in it. At least he arrived eventually, though – as manager – in 2001.

Another lad I also almost signed was Gerry Francis from QPR. This was a done deal as far as everyone was concerned. Gerry had agreed terms and we were ready to pay a fee of around £450,000 to bring him to the club but I was gutted when he failed a medical due to a back problem. I was looking for a play-maker in the middle of the park, now that I knew Colin Bell would never be able to fully recover, and the deal collapsing was hugely disappointing for the lad and for me. Francis was a great talent and he would have been a big crowd favourite had everything gone according to plan.

Yet another deal that fell through on a medical was Charlton striker Mike Flanagan. There's nothing you can do when things like that happen; you just have to get on with it. It was a frustrating time trying to bring in new blood and yet another World Cup star could have been playing in blue had the agreed fee not doubled in the time it takes to drive from Maine Road to Sheffield! If the deal had gone through, it might well have been City who carried off the FA Cup in 1981, instead of the player's eventual destination, Tottenham Hotspur.

I was put onto the trail of Osvaldo Ardiles by Harry Haslam, the manager of Sheffield United, who told me that he'd heard he was available for around £100,000. Ardiles' agent had been in talks with the Blades about a possible move but they couldn't afford his wages. I contacted Peter Swales and said Ardiles was a player I would like to sign and, to be fair to him, he said, 'Let's get over there and tie it up.' He picked me up and we made our way over the Woodhead Pass to Bramall Lane but when we arrived and sat down with Ardiles' agent, we learned the fee had gone from £100,000 to £200,000. The chairman wasn't happy with that at all and neither was I. He wanted to know why the fee had doubled and where the extra cash was going. The agent didn't have a satisfactory answer and was obviously trying to pull a fast one and, if that was the case, he'd picked the wrong club to string along. I'd been let down by the agent and we travelled back to Manchester without concluding a deal. So, all in all, we lost out on a galaxy of top players in a very short period of time. Any one of these players might have changed the future of the club and, ultimately, my own future too.

One signing I did manage to bring in was a young defender from Luton called Paul Futcher. I went along with Ken Barnes to have a look at him and it didn't take a genius to work out that the lad was a smashing footballer. Although he was a little bit green in many ways, and still feeling his way in the game, he was one of the best long ball passers I'd seen for quite a while. He was a bit of a difficult boy to get through to, though. He wanted an arm around his shoulder all of the time and if he was under pressure he found it a little tough. We signed his brother, Ron, who was a stronger character, perhaps because he was a striker and enjoyed the physical side of the game a bit more. They both got stronger as they went along.

Our 1978–79 pre-season wound up with a heavy defeat at AZ Alkmaar. We'd played a lot of games and probably taken on one too many at the end, and we suffered for it with a 5–1 defeat. Although these matches were just pre-season friendlies, they could still dent the team's confidence and do more harm than good. It was only six days before the start of the new season and was perhaps a portent of things to come.

We kicked off at Derby and came away with a point, but failed to win any of our first four matches. The results weren't matching the quality we had in the squad but there was time to address any problems as we went along. There was still a good crop of youngsters coming through as well. I'd always taken a keen interest in the local lads on the club's books and it was great to be able to give the likes of Roger Palmer and Dave Bennett their break in the first team. Ray Ranson and Nicky Reid were also emerging talents who were knocking on the first-team door and I wasn't afraid to give them a chance if I thought the time was right.

Palmer was a good striker. He played in a relaxed, laid-back manner that was often mistaken for laziness but he certainly knew where the goal was. I had to remind him and Dave Bennett occasionally that being a professional footballer wasn't a stroll and they had to work hard at their game if they wanted to progress. To be fair to them both, they got to grips with things and pulled their socks up so they didn't drift away from promising careers. Palmer had a poacher's instinct and a great turn of speed. He scored a number of important goals for us in a short period of time. After I moved on, Roger called me at Cardiff and asked what I thought of Oldham Athletic, who had come in with a bid for his services. Both Dave and Gary Bennett also called while I was at Ninian Park regarding moves to Cardiff and Sunderland respectively. Dave eventually joined me at Cardiff and would later move on to Highfield Road and become a huge favourite at Coventry City, while Gary and Roger went on to have successful careers at Sunderland and Oldham. They could have done the same with City, but they were never really given extended first-team runs and Dave and Roger probably felt like they constantly had to justify their selection at Maine Road.

With our form in the League not the greatest, I decided to add some experience to the midfield in the form of South African Colin Viljoen from Ipswich. He had good ability on the ball, but he lacked that extra yard of pace which would have made him top class. I signed him just before the UEFA Cup deadline and he started extremely well for us. There was the added bonus of him being well suited to the European style we needed to progress in the competition. Colin Bell was still in and around the squad, and it was Bell who replaced Viljoen in the second leg of the UEFA Cup tie with FC Twente – and he scored, too. We'd drawn the first match 1–1 and finished off the Dutch side 3–2 at Maine Road in the return leg.

It was a relief to finally get past the first round as manager after the first two attempts had ended in defeat to Juventus and Widzew Lodz. We then eased past Standard Liege, the former club of my old mate Johnny Crossan, in the next round. It had looked for all the world as though we would only be taking a slender 1–0 advantage over to Belgium with 85 minutes on the clock. But goals from Brian Kidd, Roger Palmer and Asa Hartford in the final five minutes gave us a four-goal cushion, effectively putting us into the next round. Uncharacteristically, Gary Owen saw red in the second leg, which meant suspension from the third round. We lost 2–0 on the night, but still went through comfortably on aggregate. We were hoping we could go all the way – until we drew AC Milan in the last 16! Our League form going into that match was fairly poor, but it was business as usual as far as I was concerned. If there were rumblings behind the scenes at this point, I wasn't aware of them and therein probably lay the problem.

I recall that a director had said something derogatory in the previous season about the way Bill Taylor and I worked together, after Widzew Lodz had dumped us out. I took it with a pinch of salt at the time, though, because there were some directors whose knowledge of the game you could condense onto the back of a postage stamp.

There was still some concern about our away form in the League and various people were giving their advice – whether or not they had been asked for it – on where we were going wrong. I knew that we'd be fine in time and that things would come around, but time was something that neither Bill Taylor nor I actually had. Whatever had been going on behind the scenes had been kept from me and, out of the blue, after three and a half successful years together, it was suggested that Bill and myself were two of a kind and too similar in our ways. These were the words of the board members, you understand, not mine. I don't know where it came from but, because we were struggling a little, somebody panicked and pushed the button. That had been a failing of the club over the years and it was happening again. It's a shame because there have been a lot of mistakes made and good people pushed out, perhaps because Manchester United were our neighbours and we were always trying to bridge the gap between us and them. In fact, I recall Bobby Charlton coming out with the best piece of advice I've ever heard about the relationship between City and United.

We'd been touring schools talking about vandalism, which was a real problem around that time, and I got to know Bobby fairly well and he said to me, one afternoon, 'Don't ever try and fight Manchester United.' I didn't really get what he was on about and asked him to expand a little, to which he replied, 'The only time you will be able to battle against us is out on the pitch.' I asked him what his reasons for saying this were, and he said, 'Well, they will always throw the fact that United have more fans back at you.' And it was true. It's the one argument that they have always won in the modern era, no matter where their supporters are from. I learned a lesson that day and that was to concentrate totally on what Manchester City were doing and not what Manchester United were up to – what was the point? As a world-wide business, there is perhaps only Real Madrid who can compete with their fame and image. Unfortunately, there were men at Maine Road who could think of little else, and now it was going to have a devastating effect on my own career.

Bobby's statement was true because it really didn't matter what we did, United supporters always threw the crowd figures back at us – even when I was a player and City were top dogs. The Munich disaster had an effect on the balance of fan numbers at the clubs, and it has ever since. It's not that easy to accept, but it's a fact that we have to live with. Still, with AC Milan to come, the limelight was shining brightly on City for a change, and, though it was a mountainous task, we had to go to the San Siro believing we could come away with a draw or even a win. The match itself is something that I will never forget. I knew it would be a real test of both my own management skills and of my team's ability. We trained in the morning and it was – at worst – a bit misty, but by the afternoon the fog had become dense. The crowds were waiting to get in and everything was set, but by 7 p.m. you could hardly see your own hand in front of your face. The officials said that we would have to play the game the following afternoon and I was delighted with that. I've always felt that the occasion of a European night – the partisan crowd, firecrackers, atmosphere and floodlights – are all great assets to the home team, and for most of that to be removed was a real bonus. Plus, we had prepared for this match and made the journey to Italy and I didn't want to have to do all that again.

The following afternoon, the lads were brilliant, and to come away with a 2–2 draw and also come within a whisker of being the first English side to win in the San Siro was a tremendous achievement. It also set the second leg up nicely because they had to come out and score to have any chance of going through. I always believed that if you could get the ball out wide and get plenty of crosses in when playing continental opposition, you would always have a chance of getting a goal or two. They weren't usually the best in the air and this was something we had at the front of our minds for the return. Kiddo was a big worry for the Italians and, with a fantastic atmosphere at Maine Road for the return, we swept them aside and were 3–0 up by half-time. We went through 5–2 on aggregate and moved into the last eight. It was a brilliant night, and one of the highlights of my managerial career, but unfortunately I had some major disappointments ahead of me.

We'd proved that there wasn't much wrong with the team, but things were at an advanced stage at boardroom level and I'll never forget the day I was given the worst task of my football career: I was forced to sack Bill Taylor as coach. I was told that the decision had been made and that a new coach was needed, but they never sought my opinion at all. He didn't deserve it and it made me sick to my stomach after all we'd done together, so I asked to be sacked as well. I didn't feel I wanted to carry on, but they wouldn't get rid of me. I had spoken with the Financial Director and told him that they should fire me, too, but he said that was the last thing the club wanted. I made a few quick calls to other managers I was close to within the game and they all said not to walk – let them sack me instead – so I stayed on. I had to get Bill in and tell him what had happened, and I said I felt I should go too. Bill said he understood what was going on but it was still a terrible thing to have to do. Getting rid of Franny and Rodney had been no problem, but Bill's sacking was completely needless and it left a terrible taste in my mouth. He was a great coach and our families had become close, too.

Unbeknown to me, there were plans to bring Malcolm Allison back to work alongside me. Around this time, a reporter from the *Daily Mail* approached me and told me he could get me in as manager at Leeds United – never say the press don't have any power, because here was a prime example of exactly how much power they had. I didn't doubt his sincerity, either, and with the way things were at City I told him that if Leeds were interested, let them give me a call. If they had done, I would have gone, because I'd had enough with the board at City, but I never heard any more about it. Having said that, I wasn't about to let a reporter get me a job, either. I would never have let that happen. I wasn't into working deals with a journalist, and wanted to do everything through the proper channels. I'd avoided the politics of football as a player and I carried that maxim into my managerial career.

The first I heard of the plans to bring back Malcom Allison was at a board meeting, when the chairman informed me they'd already spoken to Malcolm and said I was to go and meet him in Bristol and sort it all out. I made the journey feeling sick because I knew deep down that this was the end of management at Maine Road for me. I was close to Malcolm only in the sense that he'd been my coach and I'd been his player. It was never any closer than that. We weren't friends socially, despite having a great mutual respect for each other, because we were two completely different characters. I was more of an introvert and he was an extrovert. I knew that his return would mean he'd be running the show, because Malcolm knew no other way. He wanted to be known as a person who builds things from scratch, and I would have to play second fiddle to that. I'd be manager in name only and there was nothing I could do about it other than walk. I loved the club too much, though, and couldn't just walk out after all those happy years.

So I went through the motions of meeting him at the pre-arranged Bristol hotel. The media were waiting for me when I arrived, obviously tipped off by an announcement from Maine Road. I met up with him and said, 'I hear you're coming back on board' and then shook hands with him. That was it. Mal was back at City and the clock was already ticking for me.

Malcolm was full of new ideas from the moment he returned. He'd had a look at the players we had at all levels and he'd brought in the likes of Nicky Reid and Tommy Caton straight away, looking to build from there. It was too much, too soon, however, and I honestly believed Mal pitching them in too early had a negative effect on their long-term careers. They just weren't ready yet and they should have been introduced slowly but, instead, they were thrown in at the deep end and we were getting a number of bad results. It was hurting them, mentally, and when a youngster has his confidence knocked, it isn't always easy to build them up again. One of the reasons I believe the directors wanted me to stay was because they trusted me and felt that I would always be around and available for them. They knew Malcolm just wasn't like that, so they needed me as some kind of a safety net in case things went wrong.

I wish they had paid me up and sacked me.

THIRTEEN

Recipe for Disaster

Malcolm Allison was back at Maine Road and the media were having a field day. To be fair to Mal, he knew how to manipulate them to his own ends and so it was a give–take relationship. The press knew he always made good copy and the directors loved the club being kept in the headlines. My day-to-day running of the team had changed considerably, as I thought it would, and my involvement on the training pitch had diminished, too. Malcolm would take the lads and I'd wander around, watching players and keeping an eye on things, but it wasn't the same any more. I was no longer the dominant voice as far as the team were concerned, because you just can't compete with a character like Malcolm. The situation was becoming an embarrassment and, though I was still fit and joined in sessions when I could, I knew deep down it wouldn't go on for long. The board had made a mistake in the way things had been done and it would be downhill all the way from here on in.

You can't put four teenagers without any experience into the team and expect to do well. They weren't wily enough to deal with certain situations, and certain pressurised matches were just too much for them to cope with. That was the way Malcolm wanted to do things, though. An early indication that things were going badly wrong was the 1978–79 FA Cup fourth-round tie at Shrewsbury Town. It was a frosty, bumpy pitch at Gay Meadow, but it was the same for both sets of players and the match was always going to be tricky, anyway. We lost 2–0 and never looked like getting anything from the game and, worse still, it was one of the featured games on *Match of the Day*, so millions of viewers witnessed our exit. Perhaps the directors who'd shoved Bill Taylor out of Maine Road and pushed me sideways were starting to reconsider their hasty actions and maybe a couple of them were beginning to think that perhaps this wasn't the Second Coming after all.

Malcolm began bringing his own men into the squad to complement the youngsters and one particular deal saw the flamboyant Barry Silkman arrive at the club from Plymouth Argyle for £60,000. I knew Silky and thought he had enough ability to make his mark, and I reckon Mal was thinking about his new charge in much the same way he had about me all those years before. He was giving him his chance in the big-time and it was up to him to take it. It had been easier for me because of the calibre of players that were already at the club when I first came. We had Bell, Summerbee, Doyle and company but Silky came into a struggling team and the odds were always stacked against him. He made a dozen starts in his first season (1978–79), scoring three goals, but he struggled in the following campaign and eventually left for Brentford, after less than 16 months at the club.

One player we were interested in bringing in could have made a significant difference to City's fortunes in the early 1980s but, when we made our move, we discovered the lad had already been promised to Liverpool. Ian Rush was at Chester and we had received glowing reports about his finishing ability so we set up a meeting with my former teammate Alan Oakes, now managing at Sealand Road (Chester's ground). We took Oakey for a meal near to his home in Winsford to discuss Rush, and were confident of signing the lad. He told us straight away that Rush was promised to Liverpool because the Chester chairman was a huge fan of the Anfield giants. There was no way he was going anywhere but Merseyside, and that was that. If Rush had signed and showed even half the talent he did at Liverpool, he would have been a hell of a signing, but that's the way football – and life – goes, with the old saying 'it's not what you know but who you know' being the case on this occasion.

Though Malcolm's official title was Coaching Overlord, he was running the show now, which meant it would be his team and his tactics challenging for our last chance of picking up a trophy that season – a quarter-final with crack German side Borussia Monchengladbach. It was a bit galling for me to take a back seat for this huge game, considering I'd been in charge of the side that had reached the last eight. It was typical of Mal to pitch an untried kid into such an important game and, to be fair, Nicky Reid did well in both matches, but he was up against some seasoned internationals such as Karl Heinz Rummenigge and it was a real baptism of fire for the kid. We drew 1–1 at home, despite going ahead through a Mick Channon goal, and the balance of the tie had now swung very much in Borussia's favour. Unfortunately, they just had too much in their locker for the return leg, and we lost 3–1. The season was beginning to crumble and Channon became the first big name to be transfer-listed – he'd had enough of the way things were within the club at the time. Many more would follow. I can't say for sure that the bad results wouldn't have continued had Malcolm never returned – nobody will ever know – but it had been our first real blip since I'd taken over and neither Bill nor I had been given enough time to put things right.

Mal would try anything to change a club's fortunes and I never had a problem with his innovative ideas. His track record as a coach was second to none and, in my opinion, he conducted his personal life in the same way that he ran his teams – he was a free agent, able to go wherever he pleased and do whatever he wanted. That was Malcolm Allison, and he needed that kind of freedom to be able to breathe and let his creativity flow. His first wife, Beth, was a lovely woman and she allowed him that freedom.

For his second spell at City, he was married to a young girl and they also had a young baby and it was plain to see he was restricted in what he could do and where he could go. It definitely had a bad effect on him. He just wasn't the same man any more, which was sad to see. But he still tried to inject a touch of the unusual and things were far from dull. Later, when things were going really pear-shaped, Malcolm decided to bring a shrink in! This bloke had everyone in a room and, shortly after he'd begun, Asa Hartford and Peter Barnes walked out. It didn't work at all and the story made its way into the papers. For all the off-field shenanigans, the bottom line was that if we didn't get the lads to do it on the pitch, we'd both be kicked out – end of story.

It was reported around this time that I'd become general manager and Malcolm team manager, but this wasn't the case at all. I was still manager and Malcolm coach. I never moved upstairs, as they say, so reports of my demise were greatly exaggerated. I accept that the balance of power had shifted away from me but positions and job titles remained the same, which was the way the chairman and the board of directors wanted it. Meanwhile, players were coming and going at a dizzying rate. Gary Owen, for instance, was a young lad I'd brought into the team who'd gone on to do well, and he was devastated to leave the club. He was a local kid who had risen through the ranks and he found it difficult to imagine playing for anybody else. Malcolm brought in Steve MacKenzie as Owen's replacement because he rated him as a better player. Maybe he was right, because they were two different types. MacKenzie, who was just 17 years old, was a more solid, robust midfielder, but had never played first-team football with the club he'd been with – Crystal Palace. Gary was more of a skilful player but a little frail and got knocked off the ball easily. It's a case of horses for courses, I suppose. Paul Power played on the left side in place of the West Bromwich-bound Peter Barnes, another lad who was sick at leaving the club. The game was changing in that you needed people like Paul who would work harder and get up and down the pitch from wide areas.

So, MacKenzie for Owen, and Power for Barnes, in a 4–4–2 system, did look a better option defensively. The disadvantage of shipping those two lads out was that they were local kids and very much crowd favourites. It was bound to upset the supporters and it put extra pressure on the lads filling their boots to succeed. Some of the other transfers, in my opinion, were not right for the club. Brian Kidd, Dave Watson and Asa Hartford had all gone cheaply and the replacements being brought in weren't up to the same standard. In fact, the Asa deal was quite amusing because it brought me into contact with my old mate Cloughie again. We met the Forest officials in a Manchester hotel to finalise the deal and I shook hands with Brian. I was about to leave when Brian said to Asa, 'Go and phone the wife and tell her the deal is done and make sure this is the first and last phone call you have on Nottingham Forest Football Club.' Typical Cloughie, and it was no wonder that Asa, who played only a handful of games for Forest, didn't stick around at the City Ground for too long!

Another great player shown the door was Dave Watson. Dave had been a great buy for me and I thought the world of him. He was absolutely first class to deal with as a player, and as a man, and he had a number of good years left in him. The team I'd built over several years was being broken up and the replacements coming in were nowhere near the same standard. Two of the deals which Malcolm and I instigated that stick in my mind are the Steve Daley and Michael Robinson signings. We initially had a discussion about the players with the chairman but, when we spoke to their clubs, the fees they were asking were way over the top. We said to Mr Swales that there was no way Manchester City should spend the kind of money being demanded on these two individuals and that, as far as we were concerned, was the end of it. We began drawing up plans to find alternatives.

Then, one morning, we were in the office at Maine Road and the phone rang. It was Peter Swales, and he said, 'I've done the deals for you.' I asked him what he was on about and he said that he'd agreed fees with both Wolves and Preston. We were gobsmacked, to tell the truth. Knowing the chairman as I did, I think he probably sorted out the deals by paying in instalments over a period of time. He wasn't too bothered how the deals were structured, so long as he got the instalments to fit the club's cash flow. So he'd agreed fees, to be paid God knows when, and both Robinson and Daley were now City players. We just had to tie up the loose ends with the clubs. Robinson was a young, raw lad who would give you everything, but still had to prove himself at the top level. I would have paid no more than £300,000 for him or about half the actual fee Mr Swales had. As for Daley, he was worth £500,000 tops, which was about £1 million less than we paid. Daley was a good footballer, with a good engine to get around the park, but I believe our valuation would have been fairer all round, especially to the lad, who carried the weight of that British record fee on his shoulders all the time he was at Maine Road.

There was still enough cash to buy Bobby Shinton, a kid who'd been doing well at Wrexham, and Dragoslav Stepanovic, who also arrived towards the start of the season. Steppy was a great pro and a lovely character, and I had a lot of time for him and his family, but he was more of a stopgap replacement for Dave Watson rather than a long-term investment. Three days into the new campaign and Colin Bell finally announced his retirement. It had nothing to do with the situation at the club, because Colin had a lot of respect for Malcolm, and if he could have played, he would have. It was the end of an incredibly brave attempt at resurrecting a wonderful career, and I doubt anyone would have got as close to making a recovery as Colin Bell. The injury finally got the better of him, and that's the only reason he retired.

Paul Sugrue and Stuart Lee arrived from Nuneaton Borough and Stockport County, respectively, but they weren't ever really going to add anything to the squad. The club was struggling, and they needed time to settle and become accustomed to the step-up, both mentally and physically. Time, though, was something we just didn't have. The waters were starting to rise up around us and, as a management 'team', we were starting to drown. I was surprised we lasted as long as we did.

FOURTEEN

P45

Despite being told the well was empty after all the comings and goings, the chairman found more cash, or, more likely, credit, to bring Kevin Reeves in for £1 million from Norwich City and Dennis Tueart back from New York Cosmos. The team needed more experience, and Reeves was a promising talent who had done well at Carrow Road, while Dennis had seen and done it all in a marvellous career. Dennis's return would give the fans a much-needed lift because he'd always been a big crowd favourite at City. The team was playing OK in the 1979–80 season, without setting the world on fire, and was in mid-table going into the FA Cup third-round tie at Halifax Town. For those of a nervous disposition, stop reading here . . . Bearing in mind the exit to Shrewsbury Town a year before, there was always the chance that this could be a recurring nightmare. When we arrived at The Shay, I took one look at the state of the pitch, which was no more than a muddy glue pot, and I began to fear the worst.

The game kicked off at 2 p.m. and the battle commenced. They were always going to come out and have a go at us but I thought we had more than enough to see us through to the next round. As time moved on without any breakthrough, the likelihood was that if anyone could pinch a goal, that would be enough, and Halifax finally scored with ten minutes to go. Paul Hendrie – father of Aston Villa's Lee – scrambled the ball home and there was no way we were ever going to pick ourselves up from that because the side lacked heart. We didn't say much in the dressing room and neither Malcolm nor myself were the type to tear a strip off individuals. In that respect, we were similar. We would both rather think of something constructive to say, and deal with any problems on the following Monday training session. The pressure was beginning to mount and, in theory, we could have been given the bullet at any point. That we made it into the next season was a mystery.

There was something very wrong with the squad but we couldn't put our finger on it. There was an undercurrent festering away and it was obvious when the team played that there was no togetherness or spirit amongst them – two vital ingredients of any half-decent side, I'm sure you'd agree. From day one, we picked the team between us and the relationship Malcolm and I had was fine, but he had most definitely lost that aura he used to carry around with him. Most of the magic and spark that had set him aside from other coaches had gone, and he just wasn't the same man any more. Things were different for him this time around. He was older, and the current chairman was a different kettle of fish from Albert Alexander, whom he had worked under during the '60s. Albert had let Malcolm do whatever he wanted, but Mr Swales was very hands-on and wanted to know everything that was happening: something which Malcolm had not really reckoned on or ever got used to. It just made him react the other way. At the end of the day, he'd go home and perhaps have a drink in his local, whereas the Malcolm of old rarely used to go home at all.

Our form in the League went from bad to worse and we were seemingly headed for relegation. We just couldn't turn things around and, from Boxing Day until 12 April 1980, we didn't win a single match. Eighteen games without a win was nothing short of disastrous. In fact, somebody decided to take it out on our club cars – better the cars than us! We parked up as usual outside the City Social club for the away trip to Aston Villa and actually played fairly well that day. Villa were going quite well in the League and a 2–2 draw was certainly no disgrace. On our return, my Jaguar's windows had been smashed and Malcolm's car was a mess, too. Mal just shrugged his shoulders but it was the first time I'd come across anything like that in all my years at the club and I can't say it filled me with joy. It's hard to explain how something like that affects you, but things were obviously coming to a head as far as some of the supporters were concerned. It was a sign of the times and a clear indication as to how certain factions of the support felt about the way things were going. The ironic thing was that this idiot – or idiots – were ultimately costing the club because it was the club that owned and maintained the vehicles.

It's hard to motivate a team when you've used just about every trick you know to get them going, and even the double signing of Tueart and Reeves had no immediate effect on our form. Going back to the deal that brought Dennis home, we had decided to include a clause in his signing to New York to have first refusal on the player, should he decide to return to this country. Dennis had enjoyed a couple of good seasons in the NASL and had been a great success over there, but soccer's popularity was waning dramatically in the States and, when we heard he was leaving New York, we activated that clause and offered him a new deal at City. He was more than happy to come back and it gave everyone a boost at a vital time. We thought Kevin Reeves would get the goals we desperately needed but he was never prolific for us, though he was a useful striker, all the same.

We'd sunk to within a few points of the relegation zone, but the lads dug deep and somehow conjured up three wins out of the last four games, ensuring our survival. Tueart scored five goals in the last eight games, and he helped us get out of the mire in the nick of time. What we needed to do now was carry that end of season form into the 1980–81 campaign, but it just didn't happen. In fact, things got much worse and this time, Malcolm and I were shown the door at Maine Road. It is a day I'll never forget, and easily the worst moment of my career.

We started off by losing 2–0 at Southampton. Our next match was on a Wednesday evening at home to Sunderland, and I expected to beat them and kick our season off properly, but the game turned into an unmitigated disaster. The lads just weren't at the races and we were murdered 4–0 on our own ground. Taking into account the results over the past two seasons combined with this new debacle, the bullet could and should have come at any point after that. Three successive draws stemmed the tide briefly, but two more defeats and another draw meant we'd not won any of our first eight League games. Perhaps our one saving grace had been the League Cup wins over Stoke City and Luton Town. At times like these, the last team you want to meet next are Liverpool, who always enjoyed the wide open space at Maine Road. Kenny Dalglish was his usual inspirational self up front, and we went down 3–0 without too much of a whimper. With Malcolm doing all the coaching and having a major say in the team, there wasn't a great deal I could do to stop the inevitable. With the death knell ringing in our ears, we took the team to Leeds United for what was to be our last official match in charge as a management duo. There was no miraculous revival about to start and a drab 1–0 defeat in front of just 19,104 fans left us without a leg to stand on. I'd been casting any worries about getting the chop out of my head every day because you just can't work like that. I had to remain positive and believe the next match would be the game we turned the corner on, but, despite my optimism, it was not going to happen.

The next morning I got a call from Peter Swales saying he was coming to the ground early and wanted to see us both. Malcolm and I met him on his arrival, expecting to hear the inevitable, and he confirmed that he'd decided enough was enough and he'd decided to bring a new manager in. It was a case of 'Off you go, lads', and that was the end of 14 years with the club for me. At least

I was fully prepared for it, though. I knew Mr Swales as well as anyone, and I knew how he was thinking: there was no way he could let us continue because we were headed towards relegation. To be fair, I reckon he'd been amazingly patient for the past two years. The situation had to be addressed, though, before the team lost touch with the sides above and, at the end of the day, you are judged by results and ours had been bad for a long time. We got longer than we should have because it had been the board's decision to create the new management set-up and they obviously wanted it to work out. I shook hands with Malcolm and off he went, back to London, I believe.

I returned home to my family and pondered what was next for me in football. Sylvia had always kept out of football and I was glad about that, especially at this moment. She supported me and came to the occasional game, but she never got close to directors' wives or the chairman's wife because I wanted to keep her away from the politics of football. I've seen people and families get too close and someone always gets hurt, because the nature of the football manager is that sooner or later you will get sacked. I didn't want Sylvia or either of the kids to get hurt, so it was at least some consolation for me that my sacking wouldn't affect them in that way.

It was a low point for me, obviously. I felt I'd done a good job overall for the club and, alongside Ian McFarlane and, later, Bill Taylor, I felt we were heading in the right direction. Whoever put the knife in for the partnership between Bill and me had a lot to answer for. Typically, perhaps, Swales asked me to stay on until the new man arrived. Most people would have told him to shove the 'offer' where the sun didn't shine, but it wasn't my way and the club needed someone with experience to at least guide them in the upcoming fixtures against West Brom and Birmingham City. Ken Barnes was at my side and I was in the bizarre position of being sacked but still in charge for a couple of games – there's a football trivia question to puzzle your mates with! Even if we'd won 5–0 two games running, it wouldn't have made any difference whatsoever. I gave it my best shot, though, all the same. There would be thousands of City fans paying good money to watch their team on Saturday and they, if nobody else, deserved to be treated right. We lost 3–1 at The Hawthorns and, for my final game in charge at Maine Road, we took on Birmingham City. With the game deadlocked going into the final few minutes, Birmingham were awarded a penalty kick. Archie Gemmill stepped forward to place it high to the right of Joe Corrigan, and that was that. I cleared my desk after the game because John Bond was on his way and would take over from Monday. I now had to get on with the rest of my life. I could never envisage a return to City.

There were rumours in the papers that Swindon Town were about to offer me the vacant manager's job at the County Ground, and if they had, I would have jumped at the chance to get straight back into management. As it turned out, they never did, which was a disappointment because, at that time, I could have lived with a move back near my family. A few weeks after, I got a call from Cardiff City, who were battling against relegation. After Peter Swales had recommended me, Richie Morgan rang and asked if I'd go down and give them a lift and I said I'd be happy to see if I could help out in any way. It seemed to work out well for all concerned and sometimes a new bloke or a fresh voice in the dressing room can do that. I travelled down to Ninian Park for the first training session. I asked for two teams to play two-touch football so I could see what the players could do. It seemed to get them relaxed and they started playing the ball around well and enjoying themselves. I'd help on match days, too, offering Richie a few ideas when he asked and also talking one-on-one with players on occasion to try to lift them and take a bit of pressure off them. The pressure was off me, too, and I was enjoying myself for the first time in a few years. We won a couple of games off the bat and I think I'm right in saying we were unbeaten in eleven League games, losing only one FA Cup tie during that time. Cardiff offered me the job as assistant manager, but after I'd looked around with Sylvia I decided not to take it. Sylvia wasn't that happy with moving down there and neither was I, to be honest. We considered Manchester our home, and it would have to have been something special to uproot us. I'd stayed in South Wales for three months and enjoyed it thoroughly. It recharged my batteries while City sorted out my severance deal.

I hadn't been on a contract, just a verbal agreement, so the club paid me £20,000 over four years, or £5,000 a year, which I decided to put in a pension fund. The truth is, if I hadn't, I would have been on the breadline. That fund saved me and is just starting to see me through. I've kept working all these years because I've had to, basically.

A few months later, I received a call from John Benson, the assistant boss to John Bond. Ted Davies had been the youth development officer at City and, for some reason, he'd left the club. So I went along to see John Benson, unsure of exactly what he wanted to see me about. Bond had got City buzzing again and they'd made it to the semi-finals of the League Cup, as well as the FA Cup final, by spending peanuts. You had to give them full credit for turning a potentially disastrous season into one of the best in years. Benson said that he and John had discussed the vacant position and decided I was the best man to take on the role – if I wanted it. They told me not to give them an answer but to go away and think about it and get back to them when I'd decided. I did go away and, in the meantime, I was invited by the FA as a former captain of an FA Cup-winning side for a parade before the 1981 Centenary final, which City were, of course, involved in. I would have been going anyway, so it was nice to have an all expenses trip instead!

I walked onto the pitch as my name was announced and the City fans gave me a wonderful reception that made the hairs on the back of my neck stand up. I waved to them and I thought then and there that I had to have some of this! If those people still held me in high esteem after the way things had turned out recently, then I wanted to find some way of repaying them. I came home, spoke with my family and on the following Monday I told the club I would be happy to take the job. The fans had made my mind up for me and it was good to know that they didn't just remember the recent past, but all the good times I'd had with the club, too. Within a few months, it had all changed back round and I was back at Maine Road. I would now be working alongside my former chief scout, Ken Barnes. I must add at this point that I'd had tremendous support from the staff, fans and players after my dismissal. I still have a stack of letters from supporters, saying how sad they were that things had ended the way they had. Many of them said they were disgusted at the treatment I'd received, and each letter was greatly appreciated. To me, these were the real die-hard supporters, and they were what the club was about at that time. In those days, fans respected loyalty, and still do today, to some extent, but players and managers are very rarely loyal to football clubs these days. My phone never stopped ringing, either, for a while after my dismissal, but it was the time after the initial calls stopped that was the hardest of all. You discover who your true friends are then, because they continue to call regardless of the situation.

FIFTEEN

Homeward Bound

I had some devastating news in 1982, when my old friend and former City coach, Bill Taylor, became seriously ill and died within a short space of time. We'd found out that he was critically ill shortly after my daughter Tracey's birthday party. Bill was a playful sort, and at that party he'd put his arms around Tracey and given her a bear hug. As he'd done so, he'd had a funny turn and almost keeled over. We sat him down and, after a few minutes, he was OK again. He was coach at Oldham with Jimmy Frizzell at the time, and shortly after the party his wife called Sylvia and told her he'd had a brain scan and they'd discovered that Bill had a brain tumour. He was told he had weeks, if that, to live.

I went to see him at his house around the corner from ours, but things were so far down the line that nothing could be done for him, and he died soon after. It was a shock that someone so fit could be cut down so young and it took a long time to get over for all of us. I'd never forgiven myself for not walking out when Bill was dismissed, but it was something I was going to have to live with.

Back at Maine Road, I was happy in my new job and it was a great period for me as the youth development officer. I was working with Ken Barnes, who I'd always got on really well with. He was one of the old school – a real rum bugger – and we just sorted the job out between us. He did a lot of work with the kids and we had to talk with parents and teachers about the youngster's prospects, convincing the promising ones into signing schoolboy forms and suchlike. It was an enjoyable and rewarding time. There was a great atmosphere in that office and there was always good banter flying around. The day-to-day pressure of running a football club had gone but I'd be lying if I said I didn't occasionally pine for it, all the same. I may have missed the challenge of management but certainly not the politics that went with it.

We had the likes of scout Harry Godwin connected to what we were doing and, even though he had retired a few years earlier, he still did sterling work for the club. Going back further, Harry had brought some fantastic talent to the club, many of whom would play a large part in the glory years of the late '60s. Lads like Mike Doyle, Alan Oakes, Neil Young and Glyn Pardoe were brought either through Harry or via one of his contacts, and all of them arrived through being convinced that City were the team to play for. In a time when huge inducements were offered to youngsters to get them to sign up, Harry would do it with a bag of sweets! Harry had been a draughtsman and his writing and letters were immaculate. He'd write everything guided by a ruler, for neatness. Ken Barnes did a great job, too, but he had a different way of attracting youngsters. He'd just sell the club to the parents and kids but never put pressure on in any way. He'd keep it simple and say, 'We want your lad to play for our club,' and wait and see what happened. I learned a lot from both men, and would put it to good use in later years.

John Bond reminded me a lot of a younger Malcolm Allison. He was a former West Ham lad with a big presence and a larger-than-life character, and he did exceptionally well with the side he inherited. His signings of Tommy Hutchison, Gerry Gow and Bobby McDonald were inspired. City didn't win the FA Cup but the club had enjoyed a magnificent run and the place was alive again.

I returned for work the following August and Bond and Benson popped in the office to see how things were going. They asked a few questions and then John Bond said, 'You shouldn't be stuck in an office. You should be out with the lads.' I was happy with what I was doing, but they thought I should be involved with the actual coaching of the kids, too. I began going over to the training ground in the morning, then, to do a bit of coaching with the youngsters, when, all of a sudden, they wanted me back on that side of things all the time. I began working with Glyn Pardoe, who had been a youth coach for several years, and we got a good thing going, which proved to be as rewarding as anything I'd done before in football. The kids started doing well, but there were changes again in the management of the club. I liked John Bond and there was an occasion when he cut a player down to size that I can't forget. The management and the coaches were in the bath and Ray Ranson popped his head around. Ray was struggling with his form and had been dropped from the team. After this particular training session, I think he must have thought he'd try his luck with Bondy in front of all his staff. He came to the bath and said, 'Come on boss, give me a transfer.' There were a few chuckles and Ranson continued, 'How much would you want for me then, boss?' Bondy looked at him, waited a moment and said, 'A box of fucking chocolates would do it.' We all fell about and Ranson walked out, shaking his head. John had a wonderful, dry sense of humour and that was just one example out of dozens.

It was a shame, then, that Bondy quit after a heavy defeat to Brighton in the FA Cup at the end of January 1983. John Benson and John Sainty took over the team until the end of the season but, though they were quite experienced in coaching, neither had been involved in a relegation battle before and neither had been a manager. I helped out where I could, but the team was stumbling from one defeat to another, especially away from home, where the form was dire. We lost 4–0 at Coventry City, then lost 3–2 at Sunderland before incurring successive 4–1 defeats at Swansea and Southampton. More heavy losses followed at Liverpool and Arsenal, but by the final Saturday of the season it was down to City and Luton Town for the final relegation spot and, of course, Luton won 1–0 to send the club down. I sat on the bench that day, watching in disbelief like everyone else. The following Monday, I passed Peter Swales in the corridor at the ground and he said to me, 'I made a mistake, didn't I?' He didn't expand, but I got the feeling he meant that he maybe felt I could have been utilised better than I was – I had done a caretaker role before and Mr Swales seemed to realise this, albeit too late in the day. I'll never know if I could have saved City from going down, but it was hard to watch from the bench and not be able to do anything that day we went down. I remember watching David Pleat dancing on the pitch at the end and feeling I wanted to kick him all over the park!

Billy McNeill, who had an excellent track record in Scotland, where he'd won every honour with Celtic as player and manager, was next in the manager's seat. I'd also played against Billy a couple of times, so I knew he was a good choice to take on the job and a good bloke, too. Jimmy Frizzell became his number two, whilst I took over the reserve team as well as mucking in with everything else. I always felt that each new manager that came in was keeping an eye on me because I'd been at the club for so long. If they saw me as a threat, it was a compliment, but I had no designs on any other job than the one I was being employed to do and I certainly wasn't the type to go scurrying off to the boardroom every five minutes. I found I was constantly proving myself trustworthy and, in time, they all realised I was a manager's man and not a chairman's or director's man. If I ever had anything to say, I'd see the manager directly. People would talk to me if they had a problem and I offered any advice I could. I was, on occasion, sometimes tested to see if I gave information out to anyone. One manager, Peter Reid, told me he had a chance to sign Kenny

Dalglish, but he was just trying me out to see if I could be trusted. If the story had appeared in the papers the following day, he would have had his answer.

Billy McNeill was a good lad and I had a lot of respect for him. Both Jimmy and I helped him as much as we could and I honestly thought he'd be at the club for a long spell. Billy was keen on bringing youngsters through and I was still actively involved with the youth team. In 1986, our lads lifted the FA Youth Cup, beating Manchester United in front of almost 20,000 fans at Maine Road.

I remember Billy and the chairman coming down to the dressing room after the final whistle, and they both thanked Glyn and me because it had given everyone a big boost at what was a bit of a flat time for everyone. We had yet another manager shortly after, when Billy quit for Aston Villa, and Jimmy Frizzell took over the hot seat for a season. By this time, the supporters had had enough of the chairman and what they perceived to be his empty promises. At the end of this 1986–87 campaign, City – just as they had been three years earlier – were relegated to Division Two, but it was hardly surprising and, in my opinion, certainly not the fault of Jim Frizzell. He had no money to buy new players with, and the years of payments on the never-never by the chairman, who had only done what he thought was best at the time, had finally caught up. The well was completely dry. The payments on the never-never were probably now sucking up every penny and the club was deep in debt.

We were hoping the kids would come through because they were now the club's only real hope for a better future. The majority of the successful Youth Cup side were now coming through, but this hadn't saved Jimmy Frizzell, who had already made way for Mel Machin. By season 1988–89, 12 of the squad were home-grown talent and that crop had effectively saved the club from spiralling downwards. I knew the lads well and had worked with them all, and I'd be lying if I said I didn't feel something close to paternal pride at their progress. These were the kids Glyn and I had nurtured, and to have so many make the grade was almost unique within football.

There was Steve Redmond, Ian Scott, Paul Moulden, David White, Andy Hinchcliffe and Paul Lake. All of them went on to play regularly for the first team, but Lake was the pick of them. He was something special, that lad, and I've always maintained that he looked like the closest thing to being the next Colin Bell I had seen. I watched him progress from his school team to the City first team and I recall we were scared we might lose him as a schoolboy. We needn't have worried, though, because he – and his whole family, come to that – were big Blues. He would, of course, pick up a terrible injury in a clash with Tony Cascarino in a home game with Aston Villa, which looked harmless enough at the time. Nobody even gave a thought that it might be the beginning of the end for him. He tried everything to win his fitness back and he reminded me of Colin Bell, in the way that he was so focused on returning and all the effort and work he put in. Ultimately, however, he had to retire, having never fulfilled his enormous potential.

All that was to come over the next few years. Meanwhile, Mel Machin was a good coach but had a bit of difficulty relating to the fans, who had become used to larger-than-life characters over the years – myself excluded! Norwich City, the club he'd left behind (as had Ron Saunders and John Bond before him), was a million miles from the bright lights of a club like Manchester City. I was helping out on the coaching side at almost every level now – working with the first team as well as helping train the goalkeepers, and still working with the reserves and youth sides. In fact, I was busier than ever, if truth were told. I enjoyed going out on the pitch and knocking crosses in to our goalkeeper at Maine Road. It was good to walk on in front of the Kippax every other week. The youth team was where I enjoyed working best at this point and one young lad who almost signed around this time could have made a big difference to the City team if he'd developed the way he ultimately did. Ryan Giggs had been training with us a few times, and we did everything we could to convince his family that City were the team that he'd have the best chance of progressing with. But his dad was a massive Manchester United fan and he only wanted his lad to sign for the Reds, which, of course, he did, and the rest is history. Sometimes, you just have to accept defeat in situations like that, and it wasn't the first and certainly won't be the last time it happens.

Not long before Mel had arrived as boss, I'd been taken to hospital feeling unwell and my visit would end up with a cure to my lifelong vice of cigarettes. I had a bit of a reputation as a smoker, which had started when I was a teenager, and this had followed me around, even though my habit was actually not that bad. I had smoked as a player, which might come as a shock, considering today's health-conscious world of finely tuned athletes. And I wasn't alone, either. Back in the '60s, a lot of the City players smoked – it was an accepted social pastime in those days and nobody ever warned us of the dangers or had linked cigarettes with cancer. There was no stigma about it but, even so, I rarely puffed more than half-a-dozen a day. As a manager, you could double that and add a few more. I'd smoke to relieve the stress I came under as boss of a club like City, but I'd never go through a few packets in a day. I remember giving them up for a day or so once and Joe Royle telling me to get back on them because I'd become a moody sod! That said, I detested cigars with a passion. I travelled somewhere with Malcolm once and I asked him to pull over because the smoke had made me sick. I was a Dunhill man, but I also used to like Du Maurier as well.

It was a deceptively casual question by a doctor that led to me quitting for good. I'd had an infection in my toe and I'd gone into work for a trip to Newcastle away. It was a Friday morning and I went in early to look for Roy Bailey at Platt Lane. So I made my way over to Maine Road and started to prepare for the journey. I don't recall much after that, but one of the girls from the kitchen passed by the physio room and saw me laid out, shivering, on the bench. She called Roy straight away, who'd come in by now, and as soon as he saw me he rushed me into the BUPA hospital a couple of miles from the ground. It turned out I had septicaemia and they'd caught it in the nick of time. If I hadn't been found when I had, Sylvia would have been a widow and City would have been advertising my job in the paper. While I was in, a doctor came in to check me over and said, 'Do you smoke?' I said I did. 'Think you can give it up?' he asked. I said I'd never tried properly, but when I got home, I threw the packet of fags I'd had with me in the sideboard drawer and they've been there ever since. The thought of whatever the doctor was hinting at had done the job, and giving up hasn't bothered me at all.

The managerial merry-go-round continued when Howard Kendall was appointed the new boss (6 December 1989). I'd been given the caretaker's job for one game at Southampton and we were a bit unlucky to lose 2–1. It was great to be the gaffer again, even if it had only been for a week! Howard watched in the stands that day against the Saints and took over for the next game at Everton. Kendall was another man who I thought would be around for a long time, because he was top class. Good job I was never a betting man! I remember his first training session clearly; he took all the lads out at Platt Lane and picked two sides and got them at it straight away. Just simple stuff, but I could see the lads were interested again and wanted to play for him from the word go. He was a breath of fresh air at the club and he turned the side around in a short space of time. He kept me on and I was rapidly becoming an elder statesman at Maine Road, not dissimilar to the likes of Joe Fagan at Liverpool and Les Cocker at Leeds, who were renowned for their loyalty to their clubs. I was just happy to still be involved. I'd be in from nine in the morning and leave at 4.30 in the afternoon and was enjoying every minute.

Kendall brought a lot of ex-Everton people in with him, both on the pitch and as coaching staff. One of them, Terry Darracott, was youth team coach when Everton took on City a few years back, when Glyn and I were in charge. We all wanted to win the game desperately and Terry and I nearly ended up fighting on the sidelines due to one disagreement during the afternoon. After a few weeks of his arrival at Maine Road, however, we hit it off and have remained friends ever since.

I broke my leg not long after Howard's arrival, playing, of all things, a game of head tennis. I told Roy Bailey my leg felt a bit sore and he X-rayed it for me. I had a little crack in the bone so Roy put me in plaster and called the gaffer up, who was out on a bender with the staff. They were all at a fish restaurant in Didsbury. Roy said, 'Boss, we've got a bit of a problem. Bookie's got a break in his leg.' Howard said not to worry but to get me to the restaurant straight away. So I went down and, having had no food, they got me on the booze and I ended up hammered. I got home and felt lousy because I'm not a big drinker, and times like that reminded me why: I was sick and felt like crap the next day. Howard enjoyed a tipple and, no doubt, he must have thought I was a bit of wet lettuce when it came to boozing.

Things were going great on and off the park, and there was a great atmosphere at the club again – probably for the first time since John Bond. Players like Niall Quinn and Tony Coton had arrived, and we were near the top of the table. I was as shocked as anyone when I found out that Howard had resigned, 11 games into the 1990–91 season, to head back to Goodison Park. I wondered what he was thinking of, and went up to his office to see if I could find out why he had decided to walk out of Maine Road when things were just starting to take off for the club. I asked him what was going on and he said, 'Tony, if someone came up to you now and offered you the chance of managing Manchester City again, what would you do?' I had to hold my hands up – I would have had to leave wherever I'd been at, too. I suppose some jobs are just in your blood and the pull is too great.

Peter Reid, who'd been brought in as a player-coach and had struck up a tremendous relationship with the fans, took over and he told me to carry on as usual. He brought Sam Ellis in and I just helped out where needed and got along with them all. Then I was hit by a bombshell. Sam Ellis came and dragged me out of the coaches' room and took me into the players' tunnel. He said, 'Tony, there are a couple of decisions that have been made that might affect your relationship with certain people.' I asked him what he was on about and he said he couldn't say anything else at that point. The next thing I knew, Glyn Pardoe and Roy Bailey had been sacked. These were two people I was very close to and I was gutted to see them go. I'd started Roy off as an assistant physio to Freddie Griffiths in the early '70s, after he'd suffered a bad injury as an apprentice footballer. He'd learned the job and got to grips with it without any formal qualifications, so I had a long history with him.

Glyn was my full-back partner from the old days and we'd been successful on the youth side of things, so both sackings hit me hard. Like Bill Taylor before, there seemed no point to it all, and it was a part of football I detested. I'm not even sure that being the one who was 'spared', if you will, was always the best thing to happen. Maybe I had what is known as 'survivors' guilt'. To this day, I don't know whether Glyn or Roy thought I'd been in on it and not told them. I hope not, because I think the world of both of them and the first I knew of it was when Sam collared me and told me it was all happening. It hurt me to think that there could even be a possibility of either lad believing I would be in on something like that, and not tell them about it as soon as I knew. Glyn had done the kit job, too, and with him gone, I had to take on that task as well. There was never a dull moment at Maine Road, believe me.

Peter Reid lasted for a couple of seasons longer, before he was sacked four games into the 1993–94 campaign. I remember there was a lot of criticism of Reid's and Ellis' tactics and, with Reid still popular with the supporters, the fingers pointed at Sam Ellis as the main culprit. City were playing a long-ball game, based around getting it up to Niall Quinn as often and as quickly as possible, and it wasn't going down too well with the fans. The pressure filtered down from the terraces and into the inner sanctum of the boardroom. Then, out of the blue, Swales appointed John Maddock, a former journalist with no experience of running a football club, but a man who came in and claimed he was now the top man. I don't know what the chairman was thinking of and, for many at the club, this was the final straw. Peter Reid was a very loyal man and he wouldn't be told who he could and couldn't have as his right-hand man. Maddock was effectively trying to bully him into sacking Ellis, but Reid was never going to wear that, so Maddock ended up sacking them both. It reminded me of the time I'd faced a similar situation with Bill Taylor, only in Reidy's case, the club had made the decision for him, as I wish they'd done with me. So, in my very own version of Groundhog Day, I was asked to take over once again, just for one game this time, until Brian Horton came in. Brian's appointment was heavily criticised in the papers because the fans were expecting a big name to replace Reidy, but instead got somebody who had never managed in the top flight before. I liked Brian from the moment I met him and he kept things interesting both on and off the park. Along with David Moss, they got the team going again, and I thought that maybe these lads would stick around for a while. The team were playing some attractive, attacking football and, with the likes of Peter Beagrie, David Rocastle, Paul Walsh and Uwe Rosler in the side, they looked like they were definitely heading in the right direction.

Wrong again. Despite the team being easy on the eye, Horton was sacked in May 1995 by the new chairman, Francis Lee, who had returned to the club following an aggressive fan campaign to oust Peter Swales. Ironically, Horton had finally managed to win the supporters over. As the summer months passed by, Alan Ball was eventually announced as the new manager of the club. Oiling the revolving door at Maine Road was just about the only job I didn't have to do at this point.

SIXTEEN

Marching Orders – Again!

'I can't believe it. He's been such a great servant to the club, a credit to football. I feel more upset about Tony going than I do about myself. It puts it all into perspective for me. I was at City for only a couple of months but Tony seems to have been there forever.'

Phil Neal, 1997

So Francis Lee had returned to the club. I kept out of everything completely, because it didn't concern me. I had my job to get on with and that was enough. I had no axe to grind with Mr Swales, but I could see it was really getting to him towards the end. In my eyes, he was a hard taskmaster to work for, but a fair one, all the same. He had City in his heart and just wanted to take the club as high as he possibly could. He'd always backed me as a manager and I can only speak highly of him. I had a feeling that when Francis returned it would be the beginning of the end of my second spell at City. His first manager was a man I'd come up against many times in my playing career – Alan Ball. I liked Alan and I thought he was a genuine lad, but I believe he made a few mistakes regarding the players and how to handle them. He was very family-orientated and I believe he made the mistake of bringing his background into his opening meeting with the players. He'd told them about how he'd been brought up and how he'd had to battle his way to the top, but, without intending any disrespect, the lads didn't really want to hear about that or what he'd achieved in his career. The players already knew he was a World Cup winner and I think they just wanted to hear about how they themselves could improve, or what he had in mind for the coming season. I believe he put them on the back foot from that first meeting, and he never quite had the dressing room from there on in.

Both Ball and Franny had a really difficult job ahead of them. Franny had won every major honour in the game, and he perhaps found it difficult to just sit back and watch, without utilising his valuable experience. The game had changed so much since his days as a player, though, I doubt he realised just how difficult being the chairman of a club like City would actually be.

It was on a December morning, three months into the 1996–97 season, that I received a phone call from the secretary, Bernard Halford, asking me to go and see him. I knew straight away something was wrong and, when I arrived, Bernard sat me down and said, 'There's a new manager coming in and I'm afraid I've got to tell you you've been sacked.' I'd half-expected as much, but was still stunned. That was it – over 30 years of service down the pan. It was a difficult situation to put Bernard in, because we went back a long way and were – and still are to this day – good friends, but he was given the job of telling me, so he had to go through with it. The timing was odd to say the least – it was a Sunday morning, and just a few days before Christmas. It was the day before Frank Clark came in as the new manager and, for the life of me, I can't understand why it couldn't have been done after his arrival. If I'd gone in on Monday morning and he'd dragged me into his office and said something along the lines of, 'Tony, I'm bringing my own staff and there's no job for you,' I'd have shaken his hand and wished him all the best. That would have been a football decision and I'd have accepted it as nothing more. But the way it was done was difficult to take. I was told it was a Frank Clark decision and, if it was, I wish he'd had the guts to tell me himself.

That the team went down at the end of the season wasn't surprising. The players coming in didn't have the calibre needed to battle it out, in my opinion. There was the German goalkeeper, Eike Immel, and his fellow countryman, Michael Frontzeck; a couple of lads from Holland, including Alphonse Groenendijk and Gerry Creaney. They had no chance at all because, with all due respect, I didn't think these lads were adequate replacements for the calibre of players we'd sold recently.

The one top-quality player that came in was Georgi Kinkladze, and the only problem when you bring in a player of that class is knowing how and where is best to play him. You had to be a good side to carry him along, because I'd experienced something similar with Kaziu Deyna. If you got the ball to him, he would go and create things for you, and Kinky was brilliant at that and had fantastic vision and ability, but he'd never do the donkey-work like tackling back and defending. You had to create a position for him to get the best out of him but you can only do that in a quality side – in a poor team, he had no chance. Colin Bell and Jimmy Frizzell were the first to watch him play, when Georgia took on Wales in Cardiff, and they were very excited at what they saw. My first impression of the lad was that he was a fantastic talent. He was magical to watch and, in all the years I'd been at City, he was as good as anyone I'd ever seen. When you think of some of the people who have passed through the club in that time, that is quite a thing to say.

When the work ethic came in, just like similarly talented lads I'd seen in the past, he wasn't that interested. He was a nice lad, who was adored by the fans. I remember one time when Everton came to Maine Road and beat us. I saw Joe Royle and Willie Donachie afterwards and Joe said to me, 'Tony, he'll get you all the sack.' I knew what he meant, and how poignant was it that he sold Georgi not that long after taking over himself at Maine Road? Kinkladze should have been a superstar. He managed to be something very special in a relatively poor side.

The season had been pretty awful, and for the last game we were at home and needed a win to have any chance of survival. I was on the bench that day against Liverpool, and I can honestly say there was no message that came through to us telling us about any other scores that affected our chances. I know Steve Lomas went to the corner to time waste but the instruction didn't come from the bench, so if I can lay that myth to rest, I'm happy to do so. As far as we were concerned, we had to win the game and that was the end of the matter. Of course, we were 2–0 down, but we rallied to draw 2–2, having been unlucky not to win. There was huge disappointment in the dressing room after the final whistle and there were a few tears, too, especially from the local lads who it meant even more to. It shouldn't have come to that because you have a whole season to make sure that doesn't happen, and for it to come down to 90 minutes on the last game is cruel. It wasn't the first time we'd been in the same situation, but hopefully it will be the last for a while.

I stayed through the summer of 1996 and was there when Ball was sacked after a 2–1 defeat at Stoke City. I knew exactly how he felt and felt sorry for him. Perhaps if £10 million had not been needed to rebuild the Kippax Stand, he may have had the resources to bring in better players. Who knows?

Steve Coppell was the next man in the hot seat. He didn't strike me as an obvious choice for the job because he was such a quiet, introverted lad. He knew his job and was a good coach but I never really got the chance to know him that well. He lasted a month, which was a fair stint the way things were going at the club! I think once he realised the great size of the task he probably reckoned he wouldn't be able to handle the pressure, so I suppose he was honest, if nothing else. Phil Neal then stepped in for a few weeks prior to Frank Clark's arrival, but was shown the door at the same time I was. He'd had a lot of experience and played at the highest level and, to be fair to him, he was as good as gold to me. He came to Asa and me and said, 'I need a hand,' so we all mucked in together. I remember him saying that he was very surprised that I got sacked, too.

So, back to the day when I was told I'd been given the boot. The club's offices at that time were on Hart Road in Fallowfield, which, in itself, I believe was a big problem. The gym beneath the Main Stand had been turned into a restaurant and Maine Road seemed to have no soul any more. The gym had been our version of the Liverpool boot room, and its loss – in addition to the fact that all the offices had been taken away and scattered all over the place – was disastrous. There was always something going on in the gym – a game of head tennis or whatever. The place was alive and you could feel the history in the bricks and mortar. Injured players would work out in there and then go and have a run around the cinder track in the ground or do a bit of leg-work up and down the stands. All the banter that had made the club what it was behind the scenes was gone forever and all of these things, in my view, played a part in the club's downfall. When I'd been manager, I always used to get in for 9 a.m., and I'd pop my head in the kitchen to see if there was a cup of tea on and have a laugh with the girls who worked in there. Or I might nip out to see the pitch and spot Stan working. 'Pitch wasn't too clever on Saturday,' I'd shout and he would come back with something like, 'It was good enough for the shit that was on it.' All that banter used to go on and it's what made the club so homely and welcoming, but when that was swapped for corporate entertaining, the beating heart of Maine Road had gone forever.

I drove away feeling numb and empty that cold Sunday morning, having been told I was surplus to requirements. It wasn't even Maine Road I was leaving behind, just some rented building that had never meant anything to anyone. It was the way it had been done that really hurt. I'd half-warned Sylvia that something was going on and when I got home I said, 'That's it. It's over.' She told me that I just had to get on with my life and it was probably the best advice I'd ever been given. It didn't hit me until we were all sitting around the table for dinner and my daughter Tracey said, 'Well, Dad. That's what you get for neglecting us for 30 years. You get kicked in the teeth.' It hit home harder than ever when she said that. I'd always been away and football had been my life and, whilst I didn't literally neglect my family, I wasn't there for them like Sylvia had been, and there was nothing I could do about it. I loved them all dearly, but I knew exactly what she meant.

That had been my life and I was never afraid to get my hands dirty and pitch in. I remember a time when I was manager and we were in Europe. Roy Bailey was struggling with all the gear. He was pushing this big skip up a slope, so I went over and gave him a lift and the chairman shouted, 'Hey, you're the manager, you shouldn't be doing that.' I told him that I didn't care what I was, if someone needed a hand, I was willing to help. Those ethics applied throughout my career at all levels, but nobody stays in a job forever and this time I knew there'd be no way back.

When Peter Swales passed away, I was shocked, to be honest. He was a strong character with a love of life, and whether or not things just got on top of him in the end, I don't know. I wouldn't have thought all the pressures would have affected him that badly because he'd weathered many storms during his tenure, but who knows?

I waited for Franny to come back off holiday and went to meet him at his house. He explained the new manager had wanted to change things around and I just took what he said on board. Then he told me what they were planning to do for me. A testimonial evening was arranged in my honour and it raised about £12,000. That event was organised and chaired by a good friend of mine, Fred Summers. Fred is a big Blue whom I met through the 100 Club at Maine Road very early on, and my wife and I have been friends with him and his wife ever since. If I've ever had times in my career when things have gone wrong, he would always be one of the first people to pick up the phone and give me a call, which I've appreciated down the years. With the £2,000 I'd made from my testimonial match years back, I had a total of £14,000 to show for all of my 30 years at the club. Players were earning £15,000 to £20,000 a week, but my reward was less than their weekly salary. Good luck to them, but it did seem no more than a token gesture to me. The sad thing was being paid off having only six months to go until I retired officially. If it had been thought through properly, as a reward for the loyalty I'd given the club, they could have paid me to stay away from the club – do a bit of scouting maybe – just to see me into retirement, but that didn't happen. To be fair to Franny, he chucked in one of his international caps for the raffle on my benefit evening but the whole episode had left me unhappy, to be honest.

SEVENTEEN

Scout's Honour

'Manchester City is a great club and Tony has done
much to contribute to that greatness.'

Malcolm Allison, 1974

My first job after leaving City was over the Pennines at
Huddersfield Town. Brian Horton called me up and asked if I
fancied doing a bit of scouting for him and I was happy to go across
and help out. I was in fact doing two scout jobs after a short time,
and the job came with a company car, too. I never really got the
chance to get used to the car, though. I picked it up on a Thursday,
Huddersfield got a bad result on the Saturday and they sacked
Brian on the Monday! I went to see the secretary and told him if
Brian was going I was off, too. I didn't want to stick around
because I'd only gone there for Brian. I'd only been there a few
weeks but they still paid me three months' wages and were as good
as gold to me. As I said earlier, there are ways of doing things right,
and maybe the regime at City could have taken a leaf or two out
of their book.

Shortly after that, Peter Reid came on and said he'd find a few
jobs for me to do for Sunderland. He appointed Andy King and I

really hit it off with him. He was doing the chief scout's job and I worked alongside him. It was an enjoyable time and I travelled around Europe, when required, looking at players for Reidy. I did that for about a year before Andy decided he wanted to get back into management with Swindon Town, where he's done exceptionally well in recent seasons.

Thanks to Andy King's recommendation, I was appointed joint chief scout at Sunderland, with former City player Mick Walsh joining me to share the job. We worked it out between us: I organised everything and Mick did the lion's share of European scouting. He was a younger lad and it was easier for him to hop on a plane and get around. I'd done all that and just wanted to put my feet up at the end of the working day and watch a bit of telly. I did that job for four seasons and enjoyed every minute of it. Reidy was a good lad to work for because he'd let you get on with it, but when he left, virtually everyone went with him and, unfortunately, I had a few small problems on the horizon.

Sunderland are a big team, with great support, not unlike City. But they reneged on a couple of promises they'd made me. I had a private medical agreement with them for Sylvia and me, but when it came to writing a new contract, they changed their minds. If they had told me they thought it was an added expense they didn't want to pay for, I'd have been fine about it and would have understood. But they just wrote a new deal without telling me their plans and expected me to sign without question. Again, it was the manner in which things were done that bothered me. I was paid off with a month's salary and that was it. I was 68 years of age and I hadn't a leg to stand on. I was informed I'd been finished by a phone call – again. I was considering disconnecting that bloody phone! I'd appreciated what Peter Reid had done for me, because he was the sort of person who wouldn't stand by and let a friend struggle. If you were loyal to him and didn't let him down, he was a great boss to work for.

I'd made contacts in my time at Sunderland and Ian Broomfield, the chief scout from Leeds, came on and asked me to do a few bits and pieces for him. He got back on to me again and told me that Tottenham were looking for someone to cover the north-west and I said I would be interested. I recall being at Blackburn for a game and I bumped into Ronnie Boyce – the same man who had volleyed the ball back over Joe Corrigan's head after he'd kicked it out all those years ago at Maine Road. He was scouting for Tottenham and he was sitting with his chief scout from Spurs, Eddie Presland. As we were going out, I bumped into them again and Ronnie asked if I could drop them off on the M6. I was going that way so it wasn't a problem. Whether that got them thinking or not, I don't know, but it can't have done any harm, and these days I am a scout for Tottenham. I get a call from the chief scout and go and watch a game somewhere within two to three hours' travelling distance from my home in Sale. It just means reporting on any lads that they are interested in and letting them know whether it's worth further investigation. That's where I'm at with work at the moment and I'm enjoying it. Scouting is basically following up leads and being a link in a possible chain that may well lead to buying a player. It keeps me involved and I enjoy it.

Many things have happened at City since I left, and one of the saddest of all was the death of my old mate, Stan Gibson. Stan had put his heart and soul into making the playing surface at Maine Road the best in the country, year after year, and when he retired, he left well-advised people behind who did a grand job, but it was never quite the same without Stan's touch. He was always out with his wife Joyce. They went everywhere together, and when she passed away, Stan was broken-hearted. Within a few months, he died too. I miss my old mate and I'm glad to see his daughter Janice is still working for the club at the Heritage Centre. While Janice is around, the memory of Stan will never fade.

One constant that has remained at the club – and I hope this is true for many more years to come – is a man I consider to be a great pal, Bernard Halford. In our playing days, the lads used to call him King of the Cock-ups! The reason for this was that if anything went wrong on one of our European trips, whether it was the flight being delayed, or the meals not being ready on time, Bernard used to get the blame. He took it all in great humour, because that's how he is, and his service to the club has been fantastic. On a personal level, he was a great help to me when I became manager. He was very thorough and knew all the rules about what you could and couldn't do, and whenever we dealt with transfers, wages, or signing kids on schoolboy forms and so forth, he was always on hand to sort out any problems. For me and countless other managers, his help was invaluable. He was a top man for the club and still is. He's a genuine man and, for me, he's right up there with anybody I've ever worked with – and I've worked with some of the best.

As far as City are concerned, I was appointed an Honorary President in 1997, and I go whenever I can. I received a tremendous reception for the last game at Maine Road last season. It was good to see some of the old lads again and it was fantastic to walk out at Maine Road for one last time. Early in 2004, I was voted into the club's Hall of Fame, which was a fantastic honour. It was wonderful to be recognised for my efforts down the years by the City supporters who voted me in. I've done a lot of supporters club meetings with Colin Bell on a Q & A basis lately, and we're hoping to make a living out of it in the future as the new Morecambe and Wise!

Looking back at my time as manager of City, if I'd been left alone to work with Bill Taylor, I reckon I would have had at least another five years with City challenging at the top. We'd had one dodgy season and the board panicked. It leaves me feeling a bit empty and, try as I might, it is hard not to think about what might have been. I should have moved on when Bill was sacked and tried my hand at another club, but it's hard to leave a club you love so much.

I like to spin a yarn or two for the old folks at the United Service

Club I like drinking in. I tell them that before I became a footballer I was a paratrooper in Korea, and that I used to jump out of the aircrafts with a big Red Cross on my chest so they couldn't shoot me – and they believe me! I haven't the heart to tell them I'm winding them up! Crookham was the nearest I got to serving in Korea.

I do miss playing football, but take a great deal of enjoyment out of the little kick-abouts I have with my grandson Jake, Tracey's lad, who is coming up to his tenth birthday. Whether he'll end up on City's books one day, I don't know, because he hasn't really got into football as yet. He's got a great left foot, and perhaps if he gets into a team when he goes to secondary school, he might begin to enjoy it a bit more and go on from there. There's something about him, and with him being left-sided, he might attract a bit of interest. There would be nobody prouder than me if he did go on to become heir to the throne!

As for the future, I plan to wind down a bit from here on in and spend as much time with my family as possible. I don't want to leave Manchester – it's my home, and they'll probably have to carry me out of the house by the time I'm done. I've had a fantastic life in football and, apart from the odd blip here and there, I was lucky enough to play for the greatest club in the world. If people remember me as a half-decent player and a fair manager, that will do for me.

FACTS AND FIGURES

Career Record and Honours

ANTHONY KEITH BOOK
Born: Bath
Date of birth: 4 September 1934
School: West Twerton Secondary Modern

Clubs: Peasedown Miners; Frome Town; Bath City, Plymouth Argyle and Manchester City
Joined City: 20 July 1966
Debut for City: 20 August 1966, v. Southampton (away, 0–1)
Last game: 22 October 1973, v. Walsall (home, 0–0)
Transfer fees: £1,500 – Bath City to Plymouth (1964), and £17,500 – Plymouth to Manchester City (1966)

Representative honours: None
Personal honours: Manchester City Supporters Club Player of the Year (1967), Joint FWA Footballer of the Year (1969)
Club honours: League Championship (1968), FA Cup winners (1969), League Cup winners (1970), and European Cup-Winners' Cup winners (1970)

Married: Sylvia Mitchard (30 March 1957)

Children: Tracey and Anthony

Lives: Sale, Cheshire

League appearances and goals for Manchester City (1966–73): 306 appearances, plus 2 as substitute; 5 goals

Appointed manager: 12 April 1974 until 9 October 1980

League appearances for Bath City (1956–64): 406

League appearances for Plymouth Argyle (1964–66): 84

Honours as manager: League Cup 1976

Final First Division League positions as manager:

1974–75: 8th
1975–76: 8th
1976–77: Runners-up
1977–78: 4th
1978–79: 15th
1979–80: 17th
1980–81: Sacked after 10 games

Total League record as manager:

Home: Pld: 112 W: 68 D: 28 L: 16   F: 205 A: 106
Away: Pld: 112 W: 21 D: 37 L: 54   F: 104 A: 172
Totals: Pld: 224 W: 89 D: 65 L: 70   F: 309 A: 278

FA, League and European competitions as manager:

Pld: 56   W: 25   D: 16   L: 15   F: 94   A: 57

Overall manager record at Manchester City (all competitions):

Pld: 280 W: 114 D: 81   L: 85   F: 403 A: 335